ONE DOUGH

TEN BREADS

ONE DOUGH

TEN BREADS

MAKING GREAT BREAD BY HAND

SARAH BLACK

PHOTOGRAPHY BY LAUREN VOLO

HOUGHTON MIFFLIN HARCOURT
BOSTON | NEW YORK

For information about permission to reproduce selections from this book, write to
trade.permissions@hmhco.com or to Houghton Mifflin Harcourt Publishing Company,
3 Park Avenue, 19th Floor, New York, New York 10016.

www.hmhco.com

Library of Congress Cataloging-in-Publication Data
Black, Sarah
One dough, ten breads : making great bread by hand / Sarah Black ; photography by Lauren Volo.
pages cm
ISBN 978-0-470-26095-1 (hardcover); 978-0-544-57933-0 (ebook)
1. Bread I. Volo, Lauren. II. Title.
TX769.b57 2016
641.81′5—dc23
2015004574
Design by Vertigo Design NYC
Printed in the United States of America
DOC 10 9 8 7 6 5 4 3 2
4500641554

To the memory of my father, William Jasper Black,
who flew the highest kites of all,
and showed me how to reach for the moon

And to my mother, Ann LaMarche Black,
who showed me how to make the moon brighter once I reached it

CONTENTS

FOREWORD

SARAH BLACK IS A WONDERFUL BREAD BAKER, woman, teacher, and friend. We met more than twenty years ago when both of us were blossoming as bread bakers. We enjoyed sharing ideas and information about baking. We appreciated each other and encouraged one another as women bakers in a largely male-dominated profession. At that time she was perfecting her craft and developing a reputation for her ciabatta and her business, which she had named Companio. Related to the word companion, it means "with bread" or "with whom one eats bread." This perfectly captures Sarah's ongoing mission of sharing bread and sharing the knowledge about making bread with others.

I have always admired how Sarah works with her hands. She has a gracefulness and precision as she handles the dough. She knows just the right amount of pressure to apply to pat out the dough and to preserve the air bubbles trapped within. She has the perfect touch to make beautiful bread. Her book captures the essence of her philosophy: Use your hands, and your knowledge, to start with something simple and build it into something more complex as you develop confidence and skill.

Why do you need this book among all the others? Because it comes from the heart and gets to the heart of what bread baking is all about. Sarah has made the process of making bread accessible, fun, and enjoyable. She has so much knowledge to share, and she has made it available to her readers in this wonderful book.

After knowing Sarah as a colleague for so many years, we recently had the pleasure of collaborating on our bread baking school at Amy's Bread. Sarah created a roster of classes, many of which she taught. With her meticulous organization, her precision and grace, and her warm and friendly approach, the students loved her "breaducation." In addition, Sarah and I taught several classes together, and I have been so inspired by the process. It has been a great highlight to work with Sarah and to play with the dough together as true bread baking companions.

Amy Scherber
FOUNDER, BAKER
Amy's Bread
New York City

FIRST

MY HANDS WERE TRAINED IN MAKING PAPER before they were trained in making bread. I apprenticed for Dieu Donné Papermill in New York City in the 1980s, and my job was to cut up old hotel-size cotton tablecloths into one-inch squares. These were thrown into a machine called a Hollander beater, macerated with water into a pulp, and then, with an artful dip, caught by a mold, pressed, and dried.

The finished paper was held to the light to see more clearly the fibril construction and to gauge its strength for future use. Little did I know that a few years later I would be stretching a piece of bread dough to the light to check for the same kind of structure. It turns out that all of the hand skills I developed at Dieu Donné made my first attempts at bread making feel utterly familiar.

The sense of touch is fundamental in any craft, but coaxing the hands to make bread out of dough is often perceived as impossibly difficult. After all, the mix of water, flour, yeast, and salt is alive and kicking and needs a little guidance growing up. It's mysterious and temperamental and not easily controlled—no wonder it scares so many away.

As I've taught beginners and professionals alike, I've noticed their hesitation and awkward approach when the hands-on production of learning commences. Words of instruction can get in the way—there's a gap between processing information and the actual touch. But once the hands are in the dough something interesting happens: intuition kicks in and new insights are gained. Getting started is really the only challenge, and adults would do well to learn from the child who lovingly, joyfully, and confidently jumps in.

Many years ago during the Christmas holiday I taught my nieces, McKenna and Celia (then seven and five), how to make a few holiday breads. But before I had any chance to instruct, I saw clouds of flour dust whipped into the air. My advice was lost as they delighted in pounding ingredients into puddles of dough. They clenched and clumped and kneaded with fists, then patted and formed it into a kind of lumpy round mold.

They could hardly wait for the dough to rise and watched over it with intense curiosity, poking and prodding and mottling the edges. When it was finally ready to shape, they cheered with delight, squished it between their fingers, and rolled it back and forth like mad. The twisted, ragged, flattened form may have looked more like Gumby than a baguette, but I marveled at what they had learned for themselves. Their raw insistence and fearless handwork had helped them to get started.

This book guides the new baker in uncovering the inherent touch for making bread and gently prompts the feel for discovery. Skill and technique grow from this tactile experience, and with the intimate knowledge of just one foundation dough, breads evolve into classic flavors, shapes, and recipes. Companion instruction clarifies the science from theory into perceivable form, making learning both easy and authentic. Best of all, with knowing hands, large or small, the new baker becomes a bread baker.

THANKS

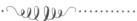

WHEN I MOVED TO NEW YORK CITY in the early 1980s my timing was fortunate; a true renaissance of dining out was underway, and my thoughts about good food were shaped by some of the best restaurateurs of that era. I perched in the coat-check room for Barry and Susan Wine at the Quilted Giraffe; I was a really bad line cook for Jonathan Waxman at Jams; I was an even worse pastry cook for Danny Meyer at Union Square Cafe (and we won't even talk about my stint as a waiter for Drew Nieporent at Montrachet).

But this all turned out for the best, because once I started baking, I fell in love with making bread and never looked back.

I admired Noel Labat-Comess's vision for making traditional bread, and my bread-making career began when he hired me at Tom Cat Bakery in 1987; we worked from a garage space located within a handsome brick building, formerly a foundry, in Long Island City, Queens. At that time, this neighborhood, across the 59th Street Bridge from Manhattan, was an unknown destination and not the popular and populated community it is now. But the pioneering spirits of Tim and Dagny DuVal, the building's owners, made it an adventure; they lived above the bakery, and oftentimes when dawn was breaking, they would lower a basket from their kitchen window to be filled with fresh-baked loaves just out of the oven.

When I opened my own business, Companio Breads, the Tom Cat crew graciously shared their ovens with me. I sold my business to them ten years later.

Since then I've consulted for many bakeries across the United States, training bakers and teaching classes for companies such as Pepperidge Farm in Connecticut, Whole Foods in Boston, and Amy's Bread in New York City. In 2004 I was even hired to coach actor Judd Hirsch for his role as a baker in the Broadway play *Sixteen Wounded*, a unique and wonderful experience. During the play he spoke this line: "It takes a lifetime to be a baker!" and I have found those words to be absolutely true. My focus on education has happily led me back to my home state of Ohio, where I have partnered with two friends, Tricia Wheeler and Sarah Lagrotteria, to open Flowers and Bread in Clintonville, a recreational bread school, floral studio, and café.

All bread bakers seem to be genetically mapped in the same way, and so the joy of this profession has been the easily made and lasting community of friends that we are. Many of my colleagues began their careers around the same time as I did; we called each other in the middle of the night as we minded the ovens, leaned on each other as we conquered the challenges of building a business in New York City, and traveled with each other to France, Spain, and Italy to taste the breads and meet the bakers of Europe.

I am grateful for the friends, colleagues, and family who have made such a positive difference in my life, including: James Rath, Dan Leader, Sharon Burns-Leader, Paula Oland, Kiera and Emma Foti, B Young, Amy Scherber, Troy Rohne, Harry Rohne, Lana McDonnell, Ann Burgunder, Toy Dupree, Jessica Blank, Danielle George, Monica Von Thun Calderón, Jessamyn Rodriguez, Karen Bornarth, Leslie Nilsson, Jim Lahey, Mark Fiorentino, Melissa Weller, Todd Bramble, Peter Endriss, Kate Wheatcroft, Zach Golper, Tricia Wheeler, and Sarah Lagrotteria.

It's also been a privilege to know the following bakers who have taught me about hard work, responsibility, and integrity, and who became my friends along the way: Dario Balcarcel, Francisco and Christo Turcios, Albelardo Ruiz, Cesar Garcia, Arturo Vasquez, and Luis Yascaribay.

I especially want to recognize Amy Scherber, the founder and owner of Amy's Bread, for our joyful collaboration and deepening friendship while teaching bread classes together at her bakery in Chelsea Market. Amy navigates her life as she does her business, with grace and integrity, and she has been an inspiration to her employees, her students, and me.

Outside of the bakery, these writers have made a difference in my career by always answering my questions and inspiring me with the clarity and kindness of their words: Florence Fabricant, Colman Andrews, Amanda Hesser, Dorie Greenspan, and Emily Weinstein. And a special thank you to Dorie, who has been a baking angel watching over me, and to Danielle George, who now lives in Fairfield, Iowa, and fashions herself as a farmer, but whose literary skills were helpful to me as she read early versions of this manuscript back in New York and inspired me with her thoughts and words. It should be the goal of any baker to continuously learn, and I am happy to be bookended, literally, by colleagues on each coast who have taught me so much about the baking life. *Advanced Bread and Pastry*, by Michel Suas, the founder of the San Francisco Baking Institute, and *Bread: A Baker's Book of Techniques and Recipes*, by King Arthur bakery director Jeffrey Hamelman in Vermont, are required reading for a successful professional baking experience. These books are an authoritative source of science observed with dedicated craft, and it helps that both Michel and Jeffrey are the generous friends that they are. My book, in contrast, is a small and quiet primer on bread making written for the home baker.

Living in New York can be challenging, but the stunningly beautiful tree-lined 45th Avenue in Long Island City is filled with friends and neighbors and was my comfort zone for many years. Heartfelt thanks to Frank DiStefano and Berny Wolff, Andy Nimmer, Carole Burstein and Richard Thalman, Miles Chapin, Carrie Levin and Bill Perley, Monty Mitchell and Stephanie Hodge, and Alex Schindler and Lisa DiClerico for always taste-testing my new breads and for making this community my home.

Before New York there was Ohio, and all of my friends from Harding High: a special nod to my best pal, Mindy Berringer, along with Andonia Allemenos, Pam Daum, Marianne Brammell, Cathy Burris, Nancy Kortemeyer, and the memory of Anne Whelan, who have all been a part of a unique and wonderful fifty-plus years of friendship. Our NYC celebration and pizza class will go down in history. And Polly Sexton, my college roommate, not only remains my truest friend, but also my favorite flavored lifesaver. Thank you forever, Polly. I am lucky and grateful every day to know that you are in my life.

My great grandfather was an architect, and my father, after he retired from a career in advertising, drew the homes of family and friends with a true perspective and elegance. I follow these men in their passion: their artistry influenced me to become someone who *builds* bread, as space, proportion, and balance are all important to me.

My mother, the indomitable Ann Black, influences me with her robust work ethic and common sense, and my wonderful sister, Claire Hanson, has grounded me with her Midwestern spirit, good humor, and smarts. My terrific brother and his wife, Bill and Suzanne Black, along with their children McKenna, Celia, and Owen, planted the seed of this book in their kitchen during that Christmas holiday so many years ago, for which I am beholden.

Many thanks to my agent, Sharon Bowers, who warmly embraced the story about baking with my nieces, shaped it into a credible query, and championed the manuscript with her steady, friendly, and welcome perseverance.

Stephanie Fletcher of Houghton Mifflin Harcourt is just the kind of editor I've always wanted as a collaborator. She has had the presence and wisdom to allow my passion to emerge yet has smartly guided my writing to the clearest possible version of itself. I can't thank Stephanie enough for teaching me how to get out of my own way so to make this book the best it could possibly be. Thanks also to designer Alison Lew of Vertigo Design for the elegance and clarity of the book's design, and to Allison Renzulli and Brittany Edwards in marketing and publicity at HMH.

Photographer Lauren Volo and I have a shared artistic vision, and her elegantly simple photographs are exactly how I want my breads portrayed. Thank you, Lauren! Talented food stylist Molly Shuster took Lauren's vision and completed the story in a thoughtful way. Shari Tanaka assisted Molly, and my ever-helpful colleague and friend Rachel Feriozzi made the last intense day of recipe testing and photographing an organized and fun endeavor.

It's fitting that I circled back to Tim and Dagny DuVal's stunning light-filled loft in Long Island City to shoot the photographs that fill these pages. From the bottom of my heart, I thank Tim and Dagny, and also especially their daughter, Allison, for graciously welcoming me back into their home, and for their love, consideration, and respect. Through the years they have become a second family to me and I am ever grateful to have known them, and always honored to call them my friends.

PART ONE

BUILDING A FOUNDATION

GETTING YOUR HANDS IN THE DOUGH

Simply getting your hands in the dough is the best way to learn about bread. The senses—touching, seeing, smelling, hearing, tasting—all leave an imprint and allow for an easier understanding of the sometimes complex science of bread making.

Before we move on to more exacting ways of measuring ingredients and measuring temperatures, enhancing doughs with starters, exploring the flavors of different grains, and shaping dough into a variety of loaves, allow yourself to simply enjoy the process without having to worry about making a perfectly baked bread.

You don't need any out-of-the-ordinary ingredients or tools, just a clear work space and about 30 minutes of active time to begin. You may already have everything you need in your kitchen, but if necessary, all the ingredients, and probably most of the tools, too, should be available at the market. The following instructions for making this first bread will be a template for all of the breads in this book.

Simple White Loaves

THE KEY WORD in making these first loaves of a white flour bread is *simple*; I'll gently guide your hands through all the steps without throwing a lot of words or science at you. Be confident and don't be scared—this is just the first step of many toward a unique and wonderful destination.

YIELD
28 to 30 ounces dough;
3 or 4 small log-shaped breads,
each 12 to 14 inches long

Active dry yeast	1½ teaspoons
Table salt	2 teaspoons
Warm water	¼ cup
All-purpose flour	3 cups
Cool water	1¼ cups
Vegetable oil	

PREPARE Organize your work space and gather your tools and ingredients. Gently pound the bag of flour so it settles before you open it, and shake the yeast envelope before you cut it open so the granules don't spill out.

If using a lighter-weight mixing bowl (the one in which you will measure the flour and mix the dough), dampen a kitchen towel or cloth slightly, twist it into a coil, and then form it into a ring. Place it under the bowl to keep it steady.

MEASURE Measure the yeast and the salt separately and set them aside.

The ¼ cup warm water should be hot to the touch (105° to 115°F). Pour it into a small bowl. Sprinkle the yeast on top of the water, stir a few turns, and let it dissolve into a creamy mixture. Set aside until the yeast dissolves completely.

You Will Need

- Measuring cups (dry and liquid) and spoons
- Mixing bowls: 1 small, 2 large
- Kitchen towel
- Knife or other straightedge tool
- Instant-read thermometer
- Fork or whisk, for stirring the yeast
- Rubber or silicone spatula
- Plastic wrap
- Felt-tipped pen
- Clock or timer
- Baking sheet
- Knives: 1 large, 1 small and very sharp, 1 serrated
- Water spritzer
- Wire rack

⧱ Notice the warmth of the water and make a sense memory of the temperature. See how cloudy and milky the mixture becomes and smell the pungent odor of yeast.

See tiny bubbles form from the yeast, and feel the grains of salt spread through the mix as they become more evenly distributed.

Add the flour to a large mixing bowl, then sprinkle the salt on top of the flour. Mix these ingredients with about 8 turns of your hand, then make a well in the center. (Now would be a good time to set aside some additional flour for kneading, before your hands get sticky!)

MIX Pour the yeast mixture into the well of the flour mixture and mix a few turns with your other hand. Little by little, pour the cool water into the center of the mixture while using your other hand to mix clockwise. Keep your fingers together as you mix, work from the center, and let the flour mixture come to you. Continue mixing until all of the water has been incorporated.

See the lumps and tangled mass begin to unfold into strands. As dough webs form, hear the sound of air being sucked in, like hiccuping.

Mix for 2 to 3 minutes, until all of the ingredients are incorporated, the grit of the salt is dissolved, and the dough forms a rough and shaggy mass.

If any flour remains in the bottom of the bowl after mixing, take your rubber spatula and, while slowly turning the bowl counterclockwise, scrape up from the bottom and mix the remaining flour into the center mass. Do this for 30 to 60 seconds, until all the flour has been incorporated.

HOW TO MEASURE ACCURATELY BY VOLUME

For this first lesson, I've encouraged you to use the kitchen tools in your own cupboards. Since most households have measuring cups and spoons, we'll start by measuring by volume. But it's important to measure accurately. Proper measuring is essential for successful baking because the final bread is affected by the relationship among ingredients. For example, the amount of flour in a cup can vary depending on whether it is tightly packed or aerated. Future recipes will require a scale, as measuring by weight allows for more accuracy.

Know the difference between dry and liquid measuring cups. Dry measuring cups are rimless, with a handle. Use them for dry ingredients such as flour. To correctly measure flour, dip the cup into the bag or canister of flour, fill it to the brim, and then level the top by moving a straight-edged tool or knife across the surface. Do not measure flour by spooning it into the cup; this encourages more air and less flour, resulting in bread that can be unbalanced in texture and taste. Liquid measuring cups are clear, with a spout. Use them for liquid ingredients such as water. Set the cup on a level surface, fill to the desired measure, then check against the cup marker by reading at eye level.

To measure yeast from a ¼-ounce package, cut across the top of the package with scissors, dip a measuring spoon into the yeast, then use the top of the package to level the spoon as you pull it from the package. To measure salt, it's often easiest to pour a little into a small bowl, then dip a measuring spoon into the salt and shake it or level it with a tool or knife.

Now is the time to coat the second large mixing bowl with a little oil so that it will be ready for the dough once you are finished kneading.

To sprinkle flour evenly, hold the flour in your hand with fingers curled, then splay the flour across the counter as if throwing dice.

KNEAD Sprinkle a coating of flour onto your work surface, then use a rubber spatula to scrape the dough onto the counter; let the dough assume its own shape.

Tap your hands in a little extra flour, then begin to knead the dough: First, pull the upper edge of the dough toward you, then push it away with the heel of your hand. Rotate the dough a quarter turn (90 degrees) and repeat. Do this 10 to 12 times, until the rough mass takes on a smoother, stronger feel. If the dough is too tight or begins to tear, stop and let it rest, covered with plastic wrap, for a few minutes, then continue.

The rhythm of kneading is fun and comes naturally once you start, but knead only until the dough comes together and tightens just a little; overworking the dough can cause tears in the structure and make the bread tough.

It's necessary to oil the plastic wrap to keep it from sticking to the dough. You can use a small plastic kitchen garbage bag, also oiled, instead of plastic wrap, but either way, you can use and re-use the plastic over and over again.

FERMENT Place the dough in the oiled bowl. Set it top side down first to oil the top, then roll it top side up and cover the bowl with oiled plastic wrap. Mark the time with a felt-tipped pen on the plastic wrap and allow the dough to rest and rise in a moderately cool place until it has doubled in volume, 1 to 2 hours, depending on the heat of your environment.

While the dough is rising, set aside another cup of flour to use later for shaping the dough and lightly coat your baking sheet with oil. Clear your work space and make use of your free time.

See the faint sheen and smooth surface of the dough as it builds strong sheets of gluten and reflects light, then gently place a floured palm flat on the top and try to gauge the layers of air pockets. This should feel a little like your cheek expanded with air, and the body of the dough should feel supple and wiggle a bit, like Jell-O.

To clean: Scrape the excess flour on the counter into the empty mixing bowl and then scrape the bowl out over the garbage; this prevents a gummy buildup in the sink and drain. Rub your hands together with a little flour to remove the sticky dough.

At the halfway point of fermentation, the bowl can be put in the refrigerator for the dough to continue its rise overnight, called cold fermentation (see page 28).

CUT, PRE-SHAPE, REST, AND SHAPE Once the dough has doubled in volume, sprinkle a little more flour onto your work surface, then use the spatula to scrape the dough out onto it, letting the dough assume its own shape. Use as little flour on the counter as possible in order to help the dough stick to itself. Pat the dough gently with floured hands into a rectangle, and then use a large knife to divide it into 3 or 4 equal pieces.

To pre-shape the dough into logs, take the first piece, flatten it into a rectangle, and position the rectangle so that the short end faces you. Using both hands, pick up the top edge and pull it past the center of the dough **(A)**, press it so it adheres to itself **(B)**, then do the same with the bottom edge **(C, D)**. Repeat this action with the top piece only and press the dough together firmly to make a tight log **(E, F)**. (Don't worry if the dough looks misshapen—your hands are simply getting used to this new process.)

⋙ See and feel how the air pockets are rearranged as you press down on the dough and bubbles come to the top. Try to press gently to keep some of the air structure intact.

Pre-Shaping a Log

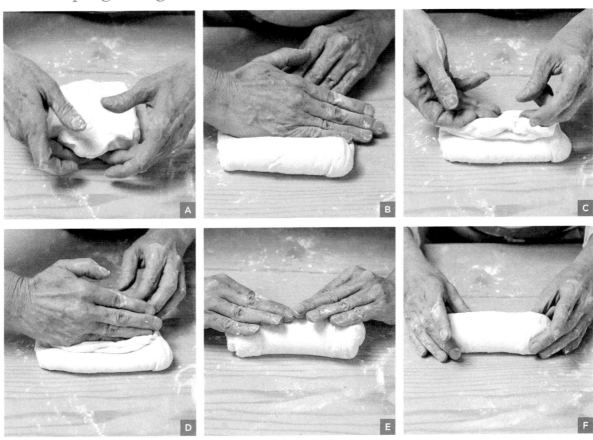

Place the log with the seam side down on an oiled baking sheet, cover with oiled plastic wrap, and shape the remaining pieces of dough following the same process. Let the logs rest for 5 to 10 minutes.

After the logs have rested, gently elongate them: One at a time, place each log back in front of you on the lightly floured work surface. Place both hands, fingers together, on the center of the log. Gently roll it back and forth, moving your hands apart and tapering the edges, until the log is 8 to 12 inches long.

PROOF Transfer the logs back to the baking sheet, cover with oiled plastic wrap, and proof until the dough has almost doubled in volume, 30 to 45 minutes.

While the shaped dough is proofing, preheat the oven to 480°F, and make sure your water spritzer is filled with water.

If your kitchen is small and the oven brings the temperature up too high (which could cause your dough to proof too quicky, resulting in a bad texture and an off flavor), move the proofing dough to a cooler area.

SCORE Once the shaped dough has approximately doubled in volume, use a small sharp knife to make a cut down the center of each log, leaving ¼ inch on either end and cutting approximately ½ inch deep. To help make an even cut, dip the knife in water. Sprinkle a little flour on top for a decorative look, and gently spread the flour with your fingers for a better-looking finish.

BAKE Open the oven door and quickly slide the baking sheet with the logs of dough onto the middle rack. Spritz water around the dough before closing the oven door.

The bread should bake in 30 to 45 minutes. Look for the color to turn from a yellow-tan to a deep golden brown. To test for doneness, tap on the bottom of the loaf and listen for a hollow sound.

Sometimes the resting process swells the dough out of shape, so before rolling to elongate, it may be necessary to tuck the dough back into a log shape. If the dough resists, let it rest a little longer before elongating.

Notice that when you make swift, confident cuts, the dough opens up evenly; when you hesitate, the knife can drag and leave a ragged edge.

Evenness of coloration tells you that the fermentation and the proof were accurate; spottiness indicates that the dough needed more rising time.

COOL Once the bread has finished baking, let it cool on a wire rack so that air can flow around it. Moisture from the interior needs to migrate to the crust, completing the baking process. Let the bread stand until it is completely cool to the touch, then use a serrated knife to slice the bread open horizontally, and look at the interior of your first baked bread.

Look for the interior to have a network of small to medium holes, evenly distributed throughout the bread. Feel the crumb (the interior of the bread), which should have just a bit of give and should not be tight and tense. Smell and taste the bread for flavor; it should be wheaty and nutty, with a light and delicate feel.

Taste a bread before it has cooled and the crumb will collapse and feel gummy in your mouth. When bread has cooled properly, the integrity of both the crumb and the crust remain intact and the texture is enlivened. It is after a bread has settled that you can smell its true aroma and taste its true flavor.

TOOLS

There, you've done it—you've plunged your hands into the dough and passed the point of fear! Now that you've made your first bread, let's pause to understand where you are and where you're going. The goal of the first lesson was for you to learn to trust your instincts and your sense of touch before too many words were thrown at you. As we move forward, you'll learn the science, the techniques, and the tools that will improve your dough handling, help you make better bread, and ultimately bring you great pleasure in the craft of baking.

There are some essential tools you will need beyond your own two hands for the recipes in this book, and to elevate your skills in bread making, but the following list isn't long or expensive. And nowadays, with the popularity of cooking and baking at home, everything listed here can easily be found online or at basic kitchenware stores.

CLOCK OR TIMER

Every step of bread making hinges on timing, and wearing a watch is discouraged when you've got your hands in the dough. Make sure you have a simple kitchen clock or timer to help you remember where you are in the process. You will also want to write down the time you begin fermentation directly on the plastic wrap with a felt-tipped pen.

MIXING BOWLS

For most of the recipes in this book, you'll need two large mixing bowls, one in which to mix and one in which the dough rises, and one small mixing bowl for the water-yeast mixture. I like stainless steel, but the material does not matter as much as the weight; the gravity of heavyweight bowls will help your cause when mixing by hand.

SCALE

A basic pounds-and-ounces scale is essential for accuracy of ingredient measurement, because weight is more precise than volume. A scale with a digital readout is even better for its exactness. If you haven't used a scale previously, note that you must first weigh the vessel for measuring, such as your mixing bowl, then zero out the weight (a function on all scales) before adding the ingredient, so that the weight shown is for the ingredient only. This is called taring.

INSTANT-READ THERMOMETER

Knowing the temperature of the water before it is added to the dough will help ensure better dough development. Buy a long-stem, instant-read digital thermometer that reads from 0° to 220°F. An oven thermometer is also a good idea to find out if your oven temperatures are accurately calibrated.

PLASTIC AND METAL SCRAPERS

Rubber or silicone spatulas suffice, but plastic and metal scrapers are so simply and elegantly designed that it seems, after consistent use, they actually become a part of your hand. They work wonders in managing dough through its many stages: a plastic scraper with a rounded edge for scraping dough from the bowl and for flipping the dough to fold, and a metal bench scraper with a squared-off edge for scraping dough up off the work surface.

LAME

To efficiently score dough before it's baked, a razor attached to a 3-inch handle, called a lame, is a neat tool. Lames are available at specialty cooking and baking stores, and also online. A single-edged razor can also be used by itself, without a handle. If you are uncomfortable with this, you can use an X-ACTO knife, purchased at an art supply store, or simply use a small sharp kitchen knife.

Equipment You Will Need

For most of the recipes in this book, you will need the following:

- Digital scale
- Measuring spoons
- Fork or whisk, for stirring the yeast
- Instant-read thermometer
- Mixing bowls and small prep bowls
- Plastic and metal bowl and bench scrapers
- Kitchen towels
- Plastic wrap
- Felt-tipped pen
- Clock or timer
- Baking sheet or other bread pan
- Pan (for steaming water in the oven)
- Water spritzer
- Lame or straightedge razor
- Wire rack
- Serrated knife

CLOCKWISE FROM TOP LEFT: *measuring cups and spoons, timer, kitchen towels, fork, digital scale, instant-read thermometer, metal bench scraper, lame*

My collection of antique bench scrapers

PARCHMENT PAPER

There will be occasions when parchment paper will be necessary for particular breads, most often to line a baking sheet to prevent the dough from sticking.

BAKING SHEETS

A baking sheet that measures 18 by 13 inches, sometimes called a half sheet tray, and of black steel or thick aluminum construction, will be one of the most useful tools you will ever buy and should last a lifetime. Most often, you will bake breads directly on the baking sheet; it can also be used as a surface for proofing dough. If you are baking on a baking stone (opposite), you can use an inverted baking sheet as a shuttle for sliding the dough onto the stone in the oven.

LOAF PANS

A simple, nonstick rectangular loaf pan, 9 by 5 inches (which can hold from 16 to 32 ounces of dough), will come in handy whenever you want to make your bread into a sandwich loaf shape. Commercial-grade aluminized steel distributes heat quickly and evenly for consistent baking results.

PULLMAN PANS

A pullman pan is a loaf pan with a sliding lid, and can be found at specialty kitchenware shops. It is most often used for pain de mie, as the pan promotes a flat, rectangular loaf of bread with very little crust.

BAKING STONE

A baking stone mimics the heat distribution of an authentic bread oven and helps develop the structure of the bread through the intense transfer of heat and the resulting oven spring when the dough is placed on the stone. A rectangular one made of high-fired refractory stone, 16 by 14 inches and ½ inch thick, makes baking several loaves easy and efficient. If you use a stone for baking, place it on the middle rack. If you are not baking directly on the stone, note that it can also be used as a way to maintain more and even heat in the oven; keep the stone in the oven, but just move it to a lower rack.

USING A BAKING STONE

If you are a beginning baker, I recommend baking on a heavy-duty (such as black steel) baking sheet, rather than on a baking stone, until you are completely confident with dough handling, and most of the recipes in this book are written this way. However, if you are comfortable doing so, you can bake directly on a baking stone, which heats in the oven before the bread is baked and transfers heat more quickly and evenly to the bread. If you choose to bake your breads on a stone, follow these procedures:

Place the stone in the oven, on the middle rack, when you turn it on to preheat. Before you do this, however, measure your baking stone with a ruler or tape measure to make sure that the breads will fit. If the baking stone will not hold all the bread comfortably, bake in batches: Transfer one or two of the breads mid-proof (and without scoring) to the refrigerator, well covered with oiled plastic wrap, until the first batch is halfway through the baking time; then pull them out of the refrigerator, allow them to finish proofing, score, and bake once the first batch comes out of the oven.

Have ready about ½ cup of cornmeal, or a mixture of half cornmeal and half flour, to sprinkle on the stone to keep the dough from sticking. Note that if you are baking multiple batches of bread, you will have to scrape off the used cornmeal after each batch to prevent it from burning.

When you are ready to bake: Open the oven door, pull the rack with the baking stone toward you, and sprinkle the stone with the cornmeal. Working quickly, shuttle the breads one at a time onto the stone and then bake as directed.

INGREDIENTS

Water, flour, yeast, and salt are the four main ingredients of bread and provide the architecture of a dough's foundation. It's necessary to build a firm structure for your bread, and knowing the characteristics of these ingredients and how they work with each other to achieve a balance of flavor and texture is an important education, one that will impact your bread in a positive way.

WATER

You may not think of water as an ingredient, yet it plays a vital role in the development of bread structure. The next three breads in this book are based on water—that is, water is the only ingredient changed in each of the three recipes to make a new bread.

Within the baking profession, bread is often talked about in terms of how much water is used, or absorbed by the flour. This is called hydration, and breads are often defined by their hydrations. For example, a baguette is a firm dough with less water (lower hydration) than focaccia or ciabatta. This is because of the dedicated shape and shaping required by the baguette. Focaccia and ciabatta have more water (higher hydration) than a baguette dough and cannot hold as firm a shape, but their slack nature translates to an open, airier texture, even though the doughs are more challenging to control.

Correct water temperature is also important for a healthy dough. "Hot to the touch" water, meaning 105° to 115°F on a thermometer, is the proper temperature to dissolve the yeast casing; above 120°F and the yeast begins to die off. An optimum temperature for the cooler water used in the dough is also essential for helping your dough to grow up and is the main control factor for healthy fermentation. In a professional bakery, the temperature of the water used for mixing can be wide-ranging depending on many factors. For the recipes that follow, the cool water temperature for a temperate kitchen should probably fall between 70° and 75°F. Refer to the formula on the next page to calculate the exact temperature, and measure it with a thermometer.

The optimum interior temperature for a fully kneaded dough is approximately 75°F. How to get your dough to that temperature is easy. Flour, air (the room temperature), and the friction factor from mixing* are the factors that influence the temperature of the water to use for your dough. Here is the formula to find out what water temperature to use:

1. Multiply 75 (because 75°F is the optimum dough temperature) times 3 for a base number of 225.

2. Check the temperature of the flour (for example, let's say the flour is 72°F).

3. Check the air temperature of the room (for example, the room is 76°F).

4. Add the flour temperature, the room temperature, and friction factor (72 + 76 + 4 = 152).

5. Subtract 152 from the base number of 225 (225 - 152 = 73).

6. The water temperature to be used for the dough is 73°F.

When the recipe calls for the addition of a preferment (see Part 3, Infusing Breads with Preferments, beginning on page 64), which may be cold from fermenting in the refrigerator, there is a new factor to consider in your calculation. Now you multiply 4 factors times 75, which results in a base number of 300. Subtract the temperatures of the flour, air, preferment, and friction factor from this number to determine the optimal water temperature.

*Water temperature decreases with the "friction factor" of mixing, which warms the dough; in professional bakeries that use machine mixers, the friction factor can account for another 20-plus degrees. For mixing by hand, I subtract only 2 to 4 degrees to account for friction during mixing. So for the following recipes, use a cool water temperature in the range of 70° (in a warmer kitchen) to 75°F (in a cooler kitchen) for a healthy dough.

You should also begin to learn how to gauge the approximate temperature by touch. As you make more and more bread, your sense of touch will instinctually tell you if all of your temperatures are correct, but until you reach that point, let the instructions above guide your efforts.

Water plays two other important roles in the bread-making process. One is keeping the dough moist as it springs in the oven during the first 5 minutes of baking. This is done by spritzing around the dough with water as it goes into the oven, and creating steam within the oven by filling a pre-heated pan with hot water.

Finally, once the bread has finished baking, the moisture from the interior migrates to the crust; and once the bread cools, the dough settles and the flavors meld.

FLOUR

Flour is made by grinding the kernel of a grain (for most of the flours used in this book, wheat) into powder form. The three components are the germ, the bran, and the endosperm. The endosperm is the nutritive tissue found

CLOCKWISE FROM TOP LEFT: *unbleached bread flour, table salt, and active dry yeast*

in the seeds of most flowering plants; it makes up about 83 percent of the wheat kernel and contains approximately 75 percent of the protein. It is the starchy white center of the wheat, and usually the only component used in white flour. The bran is the hard outer covering, rich in nutrients, and the germ is the embryo that would grow into a new wheat plant.

The protein in the flour is responsible for the strength of the dough and also influences the flavor of the bread. The protein in wheat flour melds with water to create gluten, which provides the structure and shape of bread. The amount of wheat protein in flour directly affects how a dough will behave, especially when it comes to mixing and shaping. The wheat protein level is given as a percentage of the flour, ranging from 8 to 14 percent.

Although the protein level isn't marked on the package, for most flours available at the market, different flours have different protein levels: Cake and pastry flours range from 7 to 9 percent, all-purpose flours from 10 to 12 percent, and bread flours from 12 to 16 percent. A lower protein level translates to a weaker gluten structure and a more tender product, which is desirable for cakes and pastries but not necessarily for breads. A higher protein level makes a stronger gluten structure and chewier product. For most of the recipes in this book, bread flour will be the flour of choice.

One important element to pay attention to is whether the flour is bleached or unbleached, and this is clearly marked on flour bags sold in markets. Bleached means that chemical agents, including benzoyl peroxide or chlorine dioxide, have been used to whiten the flour. The taste, texture, and color of the bread are all affected by bleaching. Unbleached flours, always preferable, bring the true flavor and color of the wheat to the bread and lack the chemicals mentioned above.

The type of wheat used to make the flour, where the wheat was grown, how it was milled, and whether the flour is bleached or unbleached all affect the bread's final flavor and texture. There are now many desirable bread flours available at the market and online; reputable milling companies who produce high-quality flours include King Arthur Flour, Anson Mills, Arrowhead Mills, Bob's Red Mill, and Giusto's.

If you want to learn more about how different flours perform, my advice is to experiment until you find one you like best, using the baguette dough on page 35 as a starting point. Keep all things constant except for the flour type, and for each dough, start a journal and take notes on the process, from mixing (for example: Does this particular flour absorb more water?)

through to baking and eating (Are the taste and the texture of the crumb and crust more appealing to you with one flour or another?).

WHOLE WHEAT FLOUR

Whole wheat flour is made by grinding the *entire* wheat kernel, including the germ, bran, and endosperm. The added nutrients from the germ and bran mean more flavor, aroma, and fiber.

Breads made with 100 percent whole wheat flour can be heavier than white breads, as the gluten strands, which form a web for the leavening process that expands during fermentation, are cut by the sharp edges of the whole wheat bran flakes. For this reason, many whole wheat breads are strengthened with the addition of some white bread flour. Whole wheat flours also sometimes absorb more water than white flour, which means you may need to add more water to your whole wheat dough.

Because the germ is high in fat, whole wheat flour has the potential to turn rancid quickly. If you don't plan on using your whole wheat flour within a week, store it in an airtight container in a cool place or in the refrigerator or freezer.

RYE FLOUR

Rye is considered a prize for its flavor, which is complex, deep, and earthy. It is a cereal grass and is sometimes alluded to as a "weed" because of its proliferation.

Rye flour has a lower protein makeup than white flour and whole wheat flour, and this affects its strength and ability to ferment. For that reason, like doughs made with whole wheat flour, doughs made with rye usually require the addition of higher-protein wheat flours such as white bread flour.

There are several different types of rye flour: Light rye (or "white" rye) is milled from the endosperm only, with the bran and germ removed. Dark rye can be milled from the outer endosperm, where there is more pigmentation from the rye berry, or it can be 100 percent whole grain. Pumpernickel, the most well-known, is like whole wheat in that it contains the germ, the bran, and the endosperm and is dark and coarsely ground. Your choice of bread and the flavor profile you want will determine whether you will go with a light rye, which is a little more neutral, or a pumpernickel, which has a distinct personality and richer flavors. All rye flours should be stored in airtight containers in a cool location.

SEMOLINA

Semolina is milled from the endosperm of the durum wheat kernel, durum being a hard wheat variety with a high protein content. Its golden color comes from the high percentage of beta-carotene present in the grain, which also imparts a nutty aroma and flavor. Translated from Italian, the word *semolina* means "half-milled," which should alert you to its coarse and gritty nature. It is most often used for making pasta.

Durum flour is finely ground semolina, so it can be confusing to learn that, for a bread called semolina, the kind of flour you need to use for the recipe is "patent durum." And what does *patent* mean? A patent flour is the purest and highest-quality commercial wheat flour available, made from the center of the endosperm (as opposed to the part of the endosperm closest to the bran).

YEAST

Simply put, yeast is the leavener of dough. It is a single-celled fungus that feeds on the sugar in flour and expels carbon dioxide in the process. This is the reason your bread rises.

There are four types of yeast to choose from, all strains of the same species, called *Saccharomyces cerevisiae*. *Saccharomyces* comes from Greek and means "sugar mold." *Cerevisiae* comes from Latin and means "of beer"; this yeast is also one of the yeasts used in fermenting beer.

Active dry yeast is my yeast of choice for this book, because of both ease of use and ease of finding it at your local market. It needs to be dissolved in warm water (105° to 115°F) before using it, and any leftover granules should be stored in an airtight container or in the freezer; they can keep for 12 months, if not longer. After storing for 3 months, proof the yeast by adding it with a pinch of sugar to warm water to confirm its potency. If it reacts with bubbles, dissolves, and becomes milky, then your yeast is usable.

Quick-rise yeast (or rapid-rise yeast) is easy to purchase by mistake instead of active dry yeast, so make sure you check the package carefully. Quick-rise yeast is added directly to the dry ingredients and requires a higher temperature of water to activate. It's specially formulated for fast fermentation and cuts the time of the bread process in half. But this actually goes *against* the grain of building authentic bread flavor and texture from a long, cool fermentation, so only use this yeast if you can't find active dry yeast (in which case, use half a teaspoon less).

Fresh yeast, also called compressed cake yeast, is sold in cakes with a high moisture content, and activates quickly and efficiently. It has the greatest carbon dioxide output of all, but it is also the most perishable because of the moisture, with a shelf life of approximately 2 weeks in the refrigerator. (It can be frozen for longer-term storage.) Some bakers prefer it because it activates at cooler water temperatures, though this is more useful for large-scale production in professional bakeries.

Instant yeast is a dry yeast product that, because of its low-moisture granules, has been embraced by many professional bakers, since storing it at room temperature is easier than managing fresh yeast. However, the requirement of activating the yeast at a very warm temperature can compromise the final flavor and texture of the bread, similar to the results seen when using quick-rise yeast.

Wild yeasts that are found in the surrounding environment and in organic flours are cultivated to leaven all-natural sourdough breads. Sometimes a very small amount of commercial yeast can also be added to sourdough breads to boost the initial fermentation.

SALT

Along with being a flavor component, salt adds strength to the dough and is a controlling factor in fermentation. It tightens the gluten strands and pulls moisture from the yeast, slowing down the ability of the yeasts to reproduce. Yeast and salt are added to the dough mix separately, and too much salt can kill off the yeast reproduction and end fermentation.

As with yeast, there are several types of salts you can use, differing in size, crystal shape, origin, and intensity of flavor.

Table salt is mined from the land. Its small grains and ability to quickly dissolve make it an appropriate choice for baking, and it's my preference for the recipes in this book.

Coarse and kosher salts are also mined from the land. Coarse salt has larger crystals and dissolves less readily; kosher salt has fine flakes, and these dissipate easily in the dough. These salts are lighter in weight and have a less salty taste than table salt, so for 1 teaspoon of table salt use 1½ teaspoons of coarse or kosher salt.

Sea salt is harvested from the ocean. It tends to have large, lightweight crystals and the strongest flavor of the salts mentioned here, and so is best used as a garnish.

BREAD DEFINED BY WORDS

Actions speak louder than words, and you will develop an intuitive understanding of bread simply from getting your hands in the dough. But words can both describe and explain some of the processes you will encounter while making bread. This helps you understand the science of why things happen the way they do.

In this book, a pattern of instruction is presented from the get-go because, although each recipe is different, many of the same procedures will be followed from chapter to chapter. For example, once you learn to calculate water temperature, you will always be aware that finding the right water temperature is essential for any healthy dough. Once you have fermented a dough, you will understand the checkpoints for guiding any dough rise to its healthiest potential. Once you learn how to shape a baguette, your confidence in working with dough will influence all future hand skills.

The hope behind these instructions is that you will learn to see with your hands, but understand with your head, the science behind the words that define mixing, shaping, and baking bread.

Making Bread Step by Step

STEP ONE: ORGANIZATION

My philosophy has always been that organization is the key to success, and because bread is alive with yeast and can be temperamental, it can only help to have all of your ingredients and tools at hand, and to know how they are used and when to use them.

STEP TWO: MEASURING

Measuring accurately gives you a consistently familiar dough and forms a predictable knowledge base to work from. For example, too much flour makes the dough dry, unmanageable, and inedible; too much water can defeat a dough that requires structure. These problems can be avoided by using a scale to measure by weight—which is more accurate—instead of measuring by volume, because measuring by volume or by eye is subjective: A cup of flour may be aerated or packed down, filled to the brim, or below the line marker. For that reason, ingredient measurements for the recipes in this book are given in weights. (For very small quantities, such as for salt or yeast, using teaspoons to measure by volume is fine.)

STEP THREE: MIXING

One of the goals of mixing is to distribute all of the ingredients evenly, so the yeast has a level feeding ground and there are no surprise pockets of salt. Mixing also begins to develop the strength of the dough. As you mix, you'll start to notice the shaggy mass evolve into long strands of gluten, and when mixing by hand you can actually see and feel the structure of gluten sheets building.

Over-mixing (which normally only occurs when a mixer is used) can both break down the structure of the dough and incorporate too much air, which can bleach out the flavor and color of bread. Allowing the dough to rest with the autolyse procedure (see page 26) protects the dough structure and flavor while building strength without over-manipulation.

Mixing by hand is, for me, the best and most important way to know your dough—from sensing the balance of water to flour to the even distribution of ingredients and the evolving gluten structure—and its ultimate destination (what the finished bread will become), and so for this reason, this book focuses entirely on handwork.

Mixing

≫ Gluten is the matrix that is created from combining two proteins found in the flour, gliadin and glutenin, with water. The properties of gluten allow for elasticity and extensibility, letting the dough grow in volume and strength.

To mix, first mix the dry ingredients (the flour and salt) with about 8 turns of your hand, then make a well in the center **(A)**. Add the yeast mixture and mix with a few turns of your hand, then gradually add the cool water, using your other hand to mix. Keep your fingers together as you mix, work clockwise from the center, and let the flour mixture come to you. Mix until all the ingredients are incorporated, the grit of the salt is dissolved, and the dough forms a rough and shaggy mass **(B)**.

AUTOLYSE (OR LETTING THE DOUGH REST)

Although it's an odd-sounding word, *autolyse* is actually an important procedure to incorporate into the dough-making process. The root word *auto* relates loosely to "self" or "same," and the root word *lyse* means to "destruct" or "break down," and that is what happens during the autolyse period. Enzymes in the flour break down the newly formed but chaotically grouped gluten strands so that the protein bonds can then be rebuilt into an orderly pattern, resulting in a stronger matrix. In larger-scale baking, this occurs more efficiently in a neutral environment without yeast, which promotes the activity of fermentation, and without salt, which tightens the gluten strands and halts fermentation; this is why authentic autolyse is done without yeast or salt. For our recipes, however, the small amounts of yeast and salt are both added pre-autolyse, and the effects of the resting period have many of the same beneficial results. An autolysed dough is less prone to tearing during shaping and will have more volume when it's baked. For the recipes in this book, I refer to the autolyse step as "letting the dough rest."

STEP FOUR: KNEADING OR FOLDING

Kneading the dough furthers gluten development by aligning the strands of gluten that bond to form the structural foundation of the bread. To knead the dough: First, pull the upper edge of the dough toward you, then push it away with the heel of your hand. Rotate the dough a quarter turn (90 degrees) and repeat. Do this 10 to 12 times, until the rough mass takes on a smoother, stronger feel. Do not over-knead: A sure sign of over-kneading the dough is seeing tears in the outer surface. This breaks the gluten strands and disrupts a healthy fermentation.

Kneading has been an iconic part of bread making for as long as anyone can remember, yet folding the dough can be a simpler and more efficient technique. Folding the dough aligns the gluten strands into sheets of dough and develops strength. It prevents the collapse of air pockets and avoids overworking the gluten, producing bread with a more tender crumb. This technique is good for especially wet doughs or doughs made with weak flours and can take the place of kneading—I prefer it over kneading for the breads in this book—and, depending on the hydration of the dough and its strength, folding can also be done one to three times during fermentation. The dough is gently deflated, the edges folded in toward the center, then the dough is turned upside down so that the seam is on the bottom.

STEP FIVE: FERMENTATION

Fermentation occurs when enzymes break down the starches in the flour into simple sugars; the sugars are metabolized by the yeasts and are then converted into alcohol and carbon dioxide. The carbon dioxide gas expands within the web of gluten, creating and filling the air pockets in the dough and causing the dough to rise; the alcohol evaporates during baking.

To ferment a dough, make sure the temperature of your room is in the range of 74° to 80°F and that it is draft-free. A temperature of 80°F or more can push the yeast to multiply too quickly, creating off-sour flavors and a weakly developed structure, and drafts can dry out the dough, causing a skin to form and keeping it from rising properly. For this reason, it's also important to cover the dough with oiled plastic wrap (or a lid, or even a snug-fitting plate turned upside down).

Dough normally ferments within a 2-hour time frame with the above temperatures. If your dough is fermenting in a bowl, look for a relaxed arc and a faint sheen on the surface as the dough reaches the top of the bowl. If the dough is tight and still flat across the top and has not doubled in volume, chances are the dough is under-fermented. If you see medium to large bubbles appearing and the dough beginning to collapse, your dough has probably over-fermented.

When the dough has approximately doubled in volume, the fermentation period has ended. To test, gently poke a finger into the dough. Fully fermented dough will retain the impression and will not spring back. This means that the gluten has been stretched to near the limit of its elasticity. The photos opposite show the dough halfway through fermentation **(A)** and fully fermented **(B)**.

COLD FERMENTATION

Halfway through fermentation, the dough in the bowl can be put into the refrigerator (still covered with oiled plastic wrap) to continue its rise overnight. This cold, slowed-down process actually brings out more flavor and

Fermentation

helps to keep the moisture within the bread. Remove the dough from the refrigerator the next day about 2 hours before baking and let it finish rising.

STEP SIX: SHAPING

Shaping actually begins with dividing the dough, pre-shaping, resting the dough, and then shaping. All of these steps rely on a dough that is extensible, and any time the dough is manipulated, the gluten tightens and the dough must rest, or else the gluten strands are torn and the strength of the dough is compromised. This is why a dough must rest for 5 to 10 minutes between pre-shaping and shaping. Depending on the dedicated shape you choose, for example the baguettes on page 35 or the miche on page 87, the vessels or tools you use when proofing the dough will also guide the final shape.

STEP SEVEN: PROOFING

Proofing is really the same as fermentation and used primarily to refer to the shaped dough as it's rising; using two different terms eliminates confusion

during the stages of bread making. The shaped dough requires time to let the gluten relax and to let the yeast activity push the dough toward its final shape, although the proofed dough should be baked just a little shy of fully proofed, so it does not collapse in the oven.

STEP EIGHT: SCORING

Cutting the top of the bread before baking is called scoring. It provides an attractive and decorative exterior, but the real purpose of the cut(s) is to allow an escape route for the heat-activated gases during the first few minutes of baking. Without scoring the bread, ugly cracks and explosive, uneven bumps can appear and make for an unattractive loaf. Use a lame (see page 11), a razor, or a very sharp small knife to score the bread.

STEP NINE: BAKING

Baking brings your dough to fruition and immediately allows you to see what steps of the process were done right and what steps were done incorrectly. If your shape collapses immediately, you'll know that improper fermentation and over-proofing are a factor.

Once the dough is placed in the oven, the intense heat causes a final frenzy of yeast production, called oven spring, and the dough rises into a transparent, gelatinous shape that inflates throughout the first 5 minutes.

As the baking continues, the starch in the dough stabilizes and the gluten coagulates, setting up the final structure of the loaf. The coloring of the crust during the end of the baking time comes in part from the caramelization of sugars at the surface of the dough. A darker crust signifies more flavor than a lighter one, as the flavor from the crust diffuses into the interior of the bread. A traditional test for doneness is to tap on the bottom of the loaf; it should sound hollow.

STEP TEN: COOLING

Even though the bread is out of the oven, the baking process continues for the next hour. During this time, the interior moisture is migrating to the crust. The bread must be cooled on a wire rack out of the pan, so that air can flow around the entirety of the bread. Not until it has cooled completely will the bread reveal its true flavor and texture.

PART TWO

BUILDING DOUGH STRUCTURE

TURNING YOUR DOUGH INTO BAGUETTES

The bread you made from the foundation dough on page 3 is your introduction to every other bread in this book. Now that you have experienced the entire bread-making process—sticky hands, living yeast, the magic of fermentation, kneading, shaping, and baking—we will build from the same formula and introduce some new processes that will allow your skills to grow and your dough to become an authentic baguette.

The baguette is one of our most cherished breads, with a universally recognized shape that brims with romance. It can be tucked under the arm and is fun to carry to and fro. When I worked as a baker at Tom Cat Bakery in New York, I lived but a few blocks away and bicycled back and forth with a leather backpack that could hold two or three baguettes upright. My neighbors were the lucky recipients; I would leave a wrapped baguette on their doorsteps—without a note, as they always knew who had delivered it—and it would rarely last until their dinner hour.

As we begin to refine our bread-making processes, there are a few noteworthy changes. Although our ingredient list and dough formula remain basically the same, for these baguettes, and for many of the recipes that follow, we will use bread flour instead of all-purpose. Because bread flour has a higher protein content than all-purpose, its strength lends itself to the kind of shaping and structure required for this particular bread. Unbleached flour is preferable for the flavor, color, and aroma of the wheat it retains and for the fact that no chemicals from the bleaching process are present.

In addition, you will get more consistent results if you weigh your ingredients instead of measuring by volume, so you will need a digital kitchen scale. For the remainder of this book, recipes are given in weight instead of volume, although very small measured amounts such as yeast and salt are listed in teaspoons. You may also want to invest in some of the other equipment and tools (described on page 10) that will take your bread making to the next level. For example, using a lame or straightedge razor to score the bread produces cleaner cuts than using a knife.

The last, and most obvious, major change from our first bread is learning how to shape the baguette. Although forming baguettes is a somewhat more advanced process than forming some of the other shapes described beginning on page 55, the heady rhythm of the "pull, tuck, and seal" shaping lends itself to creating a memory imprint of handwork, and I believe this experience, as challenging as you may find it, will be a track to follow, making it easier to learn all future shapes.

Baguettes

A BAGUETTE BEGS TO BE PULLED APART, crust splintering, to reach the tender and aromatic strands of dough inside. The very nature of the baguette's narrow shape (the name is derived from the Latin *baculum*, or "stick") shows a clear portrait of crumb and crust. So making a good baguette reveals a true knowledge of the craft of baking, from choice of flour to agility of shaping; from mastery of fermentation to deftness of scoring. This may seem like a lot of pressure for a beginner, but there's no better way to learn than by doing, and there is no better model of education than the baguette.

YIELD
28 to 30 ounces dough;
3 or 4 small baguettes, each 12 to
14 inches long

Active dry yeast	1½ teaspoons
Table salt	2 teaspoons
Warm water	1.75 ounces
Unbleached bread flour	16 ounces
Cool water	10 ounces
Vegetable oil	

What's New

- Bread flour replaces all-purpose flour.
- Ingredients are weighed instead of measured by volume.
- The dough is autolysed and folded.
- The dough is shaped into baguettes and proofed with a cloth structure.
- The baguettes are scored with a lame or razor and with four cuts.

PREPARE Organize your work space and gather your tools and ingredients.

MEASURE AND WEIGH Measure the yeast and the salt separately and set them aside. (Note: With these small quantities, it is simply easier to measure the yeast and salt in teaspoons instead of by weight.)

Weigh the warm water into a small bowl. The warm water should feel hot to the touch, between 105° and 115°F. Sprinkle the yeast on top of the water, stir to dissolve, and set aside.

To accurately weigh the ingredients, the vessel holding them must first be placed on the scale and then zeroed out, called taring, before the ingredients are added and weighed.

Weigh the flour into a large mixing bowl. Sprinkle the salt on top of the flour, stir to incorporate, and then make a well in the center.

To measure water at the right temperature, add lukewarm water to any large container as a starting point. Little by little, add cool or hot water until you arrive at a temperature of 70° to 75°F, then weigh the amount you need from this supply. This method is easier than trying to get the exact reading and amount directly from your faucet and also prevents wasting water.

Weigh the cool water into a small bowl. The cool water temperature should be between 70° and 75°F. You can either calculate the exact water temperature needed and measure it with a thermometer, as described on page 17, or learn to gauge the acceptable range by touch.

MIX Add the yeast mixture to the flour, stir 3 or 4 turns, then, little by little, add the cool water. Mix with your hands, keeping your fingers together as you mix in a clockwise direction, pouring the water into the middle and working from the center, letting the flour mixture come to you. Mix for 2 to 3 minutes, until all of the ingredients are incorporated, the grit of the salt is dissolved, and the dough forms a rough and shaggy mass, then stop mixing.

Since flour absorptions differ, or if you are working in a cold or dry environment, you may need to add up to 1 ounce more water if your dough feels too dry.

LET THE DOUGH REST (AUTOLYSE) Cover the bowl with a kitchen towel or plastic wrap and let the dough stand still for about 30 minutes. (In professional kitchens, this is known as autolyse.)

Note the differences in the dough's appearance once the autolyse period is over: The dough will have a more developed structure, reflecting the alignment of the gluten strands and the strength of the gluten matrix.

FOLD Sprinkle your work surface with flour and then use a plastic bowl scraper to scrape the dough out onto it. Tap your hands in a little flour, then gently flatten the dough into a rectangle, with the short side facing you. Note that folding (see page 56) will take the place of kneading in this recipe because it is an efficient way to build strength without making the bread tough from overworking the gluten.

Once folded, see and feel how the dough immediately and almost magically changes from rough and broken to smooth and strong.

Use your fingers or the plastic scraper to flip the top edge of the dough down to just below the center, then flip the bottom edge up to just above the center. Repeat this process for the right and left sides, then turn the dough over and dust off the flour.

FERMENT Oil a second large bowl, then place the dough in it, seam side up, to oil the top. Then turn it seam side down, and cover the bowl with oiled plastic wrap. Mark the time with a felt-tipped pen on the plastic wrap and allow the dough to rest and rise in a moderately cool place until it has doubled in volume, 1 to 2 hours, depending on the heat of your environment.

CUT, PRE-SHAPE, REST, AND SHAPE Once the dough has doubled in volume, sprinkle a little more flour onto your work surface, then scrape the dough out onto it and let the dough assume its natural shape. Dust the top of the dough with a little flour and pat it down gently, then use a metal bench scraper or knife to divide it into 3 or 4 equal pieces.

To pre-shape a baguette, start with the same basic log structure as on page 7: Pat each piece of dough into a rectangle shape with the short end toward you. Use your fingers to lift and pull the top edge of the dough down to just below the center. Now, press that edge very gently into the dough, then lift and pull the bottom edge up to just above the center, and press that edge down. Fold this shape in half to form a log. Turn the log over so the seam side is down on the table. This log shape is the first step in making a baguette.

After all the pieces are shaped into logs, cover them with oiled plastic wrap and let them rest for 5 to 10 minutes before you continue shaping.

When the rest period is finished, sprinkle just a bit more flour on the counter, then take one log and position it lengthwise in front of you with the bottom seam facing up.

Begin by folding the dough in half (see **(A)**, next page), using the heel of your hand to make an imprint of the crease before folding. Starting from the upper right tip of the dough, pull and stretch the dough over and down between the thumb and fingers of your left hand, then seal it with the bottom of the palm of your right hand **(B)**. Continue this process all the way down the length of the baguette. Your right palm should be held upright, like waving, so it does not flatten and compress the dough. Repeat this process once or even twice more, until the baguette is approximately 1½ inches wide **(C, D)**.

A baguette is the most challenging of all shapes, and although the instructions for forming it seem complicated, with practice your instincts will kick in. The two-handed movement of pulling, tucking, and sealing the dough into a long cylinder becomes a rhythmic process and one of those heady moments that define the craft of bread making—you'll see.

Shaping a Baguette

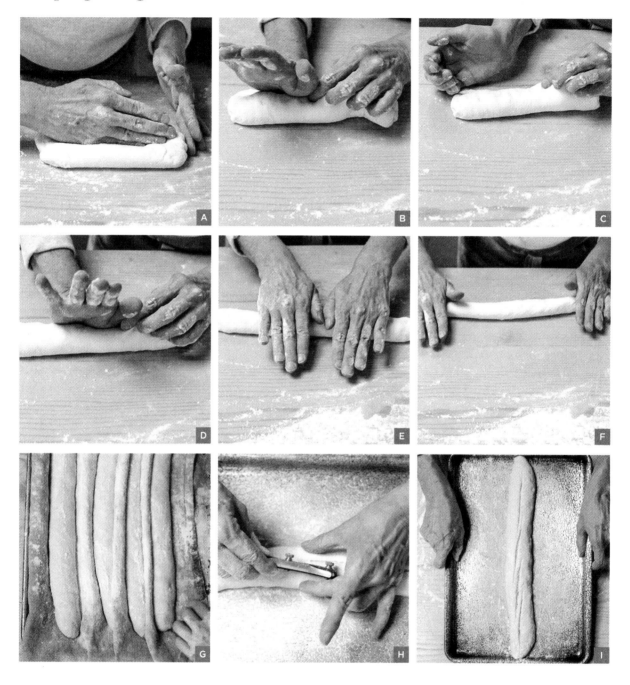

Set the baguette aside, covered with oiled plastic wrap, and repeat the process with the remaining pieces of dough, setting each one aside under the plastic wrap as you finish. Once all the pieces are shaped, let them rest, covered, for another 8 to 10 minutes.

After the dough has rested, elongate the baguettes on a very lightly floured counter: Place 1 baguette in front of you, lengthwise. Use both hands, with your fingers together, to roll the baguette back and forth, starting in the center **(E)** and then moving your hands apart and tapering the edges until the baguette is 12 to 14 inches long **(F)**. Repeat with the remaining baguettes.

PROOF To proof the baguettes, take a kitchen towel about the size of your baking sheet, and place it on top of the baking sheet. Tuck the left edge of the towel under itself, then sprinkle the entire towel heavily with flour. Place the first baguette, seam side down, on top of the towel at the very left end. Pull the towel on the right toward the baguette to form a loop up against the dough. Place the second baguette on the towel, and pull the towel to make another loop. Repeat with the third and fourth baguettes and finish by tucking the right-hand edge of the towel under itself to form a light structure for the last baguette **(G)**. Cover with oiled plastic wrap and let the baguettes proof until the dough has doubled in volume, 30 to 45 minutes.

While the shaped dough is proofing, preheat the oven to 480°F, with an empty pan for creating steam on the bottom of the oven. Have ready a spritzer filled with water near the oven and approximately 8 ounces of hot water to pour into the empty pan.

SCORE Once the baguettes have approximately doubled in volume, transfer them from the towel to an oiled baking sheet and place 2 to 3 inches apart, then dust a little flour on top for a decorative look and smooth the flour gently with your hand. To score the dough, hold a lame or straightedge razor between your thumb and forefinger. Dip the lame or razor in water, and then try to keep the blade at a slight angle as you quickly slice into the dough. Score each baguette with 4 cuts down the center as shown on the following page, leaving ¼ inch at either end and cutting approximately ½ inch deep **(H, I)**.

By utilizing kitchen towels as described above, you're essentially making your own homemade *couche*. Meaning "layer" in French, a couche is a heavy linen cloth traditionally used by professionals to frame the shape of baguettes as they proof. This helps to keep the shape intact. The word can also be used as a verb, referring to the process itself.

※》 The baguettes should be scored as pictured. Before you score a baguette, draw four baguette shapes on a piece of paper, and practice drawing the cuts.

BAKE Open the oven door, and, working quickly, slide the baking sheet with the baguettes onto the middle rack and pour the hot water into the empty pan below to create steam before quickly closing the oven door. Be careful to avert your face when adding the water so as not to burn yourself with the burst of steam. After 1 minute, open the oven door and spritz around the dough with water, then close the door again.

The dough should spring into form very quickly from the immediate transfer of heat. As much fun as this is to behold, try not to open the oven door too often, as each time you do there will be a significant heat loss of 25° to 50°F, and this heat loss will affect the oven spring of the baking bread. However, most ovens have hot spots, so go ahead and move your bread around if the crust is browning too quickly in some areas.

The baguettes should bake in 35 to 45 minutes and develop an even dark reddish brown color. They should be particularly brown around the bloom from the cuts.

COOL Let the baguettes cool to the touch on a wire rack before cutting into them. As they cool, the moisture from the interior will migrate to the crust, completing the baking process.

The differences between this bread and the bread in Part 1 might not be immediately obvious to the untrained eye, though you can now count on the accuracy of your measurements to make a well-balanced dough. The couche cloth helped to form a true, rounded baguette structure, and the cut from the lame was probably swifter and left a cleaner look than the knife cut. The volume should be greater and the crust should have a sheen to it due to the increased steam in the oven during the initial stages of baking. Most important, if you used unbleached flour, this will have influenced the taste of the bread and the color of the crumb to be truer to the taste and color of the wheat.

ADDING WATER TO MAKE FOCACCIA

Focaccia, which comes from the Latin *focus*, meaning "center" or "hearth," is a bread that I love to make for family and friends, and when I do it truly does become the "focus" of my kitchen, dinner, and conversation.

Focaccia is a versatile dough because it incorporates a bit more water than the baguette; it has enough structure to loosely hold a boule or batard shape, but it also has enough give to spread like a pizza. The extra water contributes to a moist crumb with a network of larger holes.

As you will begin to see, the more water in the dough, the harder it can be to handle. This dough (and the ciabatta that follows) pours from the bowl, sticks to your hands, and covers your counter like lava from a volcano—you need to be quick to keep it in line. But the drastic changes in dough consistency of the focaccia in this chapter, and the ciabatta in the following chapter, will enable you to immediately feel different dough structures. Most important, it will give your hands the kind of training that will improve all of your future dough handling.

Focaccia

YIELD
Approximately 30 ounces dough;
One 17-by-11-inch rectangle

FOCACCIA CAN BE THE CANVAS for any variety of toppings, flavors, and textures. My favorites are the ingredients that are simple enough to enhance the flavor of the bread, like a good olive oil and a handful of fresh herbs tossed with a little crunchy coarse salt. For this recipe, you will need an 18-by-13-inch rimmed baking sheet, also called a half sheet pan, or one in a similar size. The dough can also be shaped into rolls (page 80), breadsticks (page 74), or into pizza rounds (substituting focaccia dough for the ciabatta, page 161).

Active dry yeast	1½ teaspoons
Table salt	2 teaspoons
Warm water	1.75 ounces
Unbleached bread flour	16 ounces
Cool water	11.5 ounces
Vegetable oil	
Olive oil	2 tablespoons, plus more for the baking sheet
Dried tarragon	2 tablespoons
Coarse salt	1 tablespoon

MEASURE AND WEIGH Measure the yeast and the table salt separately and set them aside.

Weigh the warm water into a small bowl. It should feel hot to the touch, between 105° and 115°F. Sprinkle the yeast on top of the water, stir to dissolve, and set aside.

What's New

- The dough incorporates more water.
- The dough is softer and looser in structure/texture.
- Fermentation and proof times can be shorter.
- The dough is topped with ingredients and baked in a pan.

Weigh the flour into a large mixing bowl. Sprinkle the table salt on top of the flour, stir to incorporate, and then make a well in the center.

Weigh the cool water into a small bowl. The cool water temperature should be between 70° and 75°F. Refer to page 17 to calculate the exact temperature and measure it with a thermometer, or gauge the approximate temperature by touch.

MIX Add the yeast mixture to the flour, stir 3 or 4 turns, then, little by little, add the cool water. Mix with your hands for 2 to 3 minutes, until all of the ingredients are incorporated, the grit of the salt is dissolved, and the dough forms a rough and shaggy mass, and then stop.

LET THE DOUGH REST Cover the bowl with a kitchen towel or plastic wrap and let the dough stand still for about 30 minutes.

FOLD Sprinkle your work surface with flour and then use a plastic bowl scraper to scrape the dough out onto it. Tap your hands in a little flour, then gently flatten the dough into a rectangle, with the short side facing you.

Use your fingers or the plastic scraper to flip the top edge of the dough down to just below the center, then flip the bottom edge up to just above the center. Repeat this process for the right and left sides, then turn the dough over and dust off the flour.

FERMENT Oil a second large bowl with vegetable oil, then place the dough in it, seam side up, to oil the top. Then turn it seam side down, and cover the bowl with oiled plastic wrap. Mark the time with a felt-tipped pen on the plastic wrap and allow the dough to rest and rise in a moderately cool place until it has doubled in volume, 1 to 2 hours, depending on the heat of your environment.

SHAPE Once the dough has doubled in volume, oil an 18-by-13-inch rimmed baking sheet with olive oil and scrape the dough onto it, letting the dough relax into its own shape.

⇒ Your choice of flour, be it all-purpose or bread flour, or one particular brand instead of another, will determine the water absorption—some flours absorb more water than others. If your dough feels overly dry, add another ounce or two of water.

⇒ This wet dough is more vulnerable to warm temperatures and may ferment more quickly than the baguette dough. Check it after 1 hour to see where it is in the fermentation process.

Because of the resting period of the dough and the folding, which add both strength and alignment to the gluten structure, this dough should have body and be extensible—note how forgiving it is when you stretch it. If the dough is *not* forgiving, don't force it; let it rest and relax for 5 to 8 more minutes, then try again.

Drizzle 2 tablespoons olive oil over the top of the dough, then use your fingertips to gently press and dimple the dough, distributing the oil and stretching and pushing the dough evenly into the corners of the baking sheet.

PROOF Because your dough is topped with olive oil, it does not need to be covered. Let it proof on the baking sheet until doubled in volume, 30 to 45 minutes.

While the dough is proofing, preheat the oven to 450°F, with a rack in the middle for baking and an empty pan for creating steam on the bottom of the oven. Have ready a spritzer filled with water near the oven, and approximately 8 ounces of hot water to pour into the empty pan.

BAKE Once the shaped dough has approximately doubled in volume, again use your fingertips to make dimples all over the dough. Sprinkle the tarragon and then the coarse salt across the top and press the ingredients gently into the dough.

Slide the baking sheet into the oven, and pour the hot water into the empty pan below to create steam before quickly closing the oven door.

The focaccia should bake to a golden brown in 35 to 45 minutes, with bubbles and blisters and shimmering pools of oil.

COOL Let the focaccia cool for 10 minutes in the baking sheet, then remove it from the pan and let it cool completely on a wire rack.

The differences between this bread and the baguette will be obvious: Because of the extra water in the dough and the gentler methods of dough manipulation, the crumb of the focaccia will be more open, airy, elastic, and tender, and will also be redolent of olive oil and tarragon, with the crunch of salt crystals.

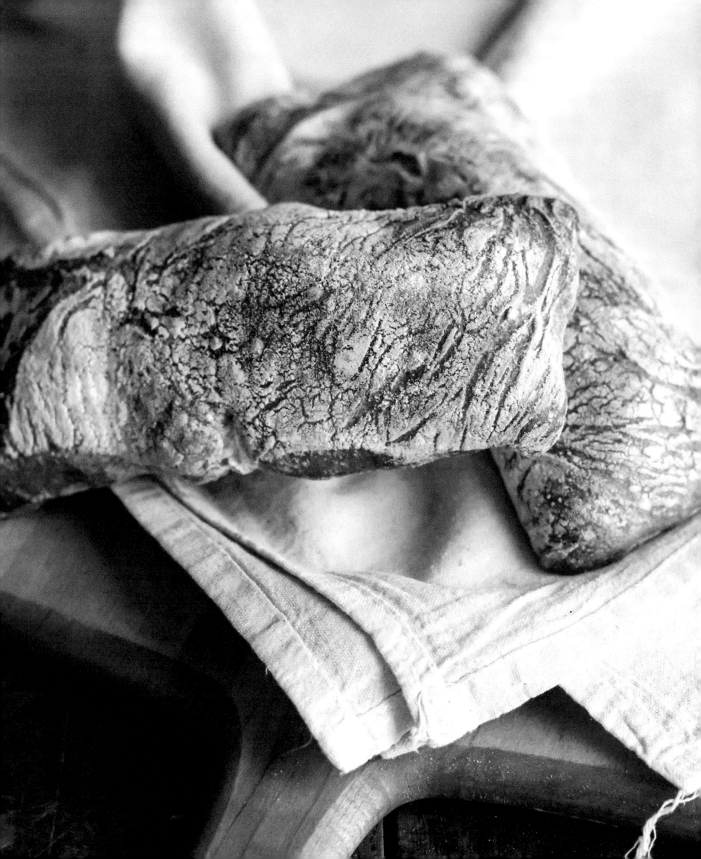

ADDING MORE WATER TO MAKE CIABATTA

Ciabatta is known for its high proportion of water to flour, and the amount of water gives the bread its rough, slack shape (*ciabatta* means "slipper" in Italian). Here is where the additional ounce or two of water is going to make a drastic difference in the way you manipulate the dough, and in the bread's final appearance: The interior structure will be a lovely network of large holes surrounded by lacy strands of bread.

I am known for my big, domed ciabatta, which I introduced to the New York City marketplace way back in the 1990s as a cornerstone of my bread-making business—but the easiest ciabatta shape to manage is the familiar long, flat rectangle, which can serve for making all kinds of sandwiches or for dipping into hearty soups and stews. The dough itself can also be the basis for pizza dough (page 161) and even crackers (page 163).

Making ciabatta for the first time may feel like an impossibly sticky and messy process, but have faith and don't be scared—the work is worth the results, as ciabatta is a true pleasure to behold and an even greater pleasure to eat.

Ciabatta

YIELD
Approximately 32 ounces dough;
4 small rectangular loaves, each
approximately 8 by 4 inches

I LOVE TO GET MY HANDS IN CIABATTA. The soupy, sticky dough pours like pancake batter from the bowl and almost oozes off the kitchen counter, seemingly impossible to handle. I gingerly shuffle a plastic scraper under the ever-expanding edge, then lift and, with a snap of my wrist, flick it over on top of itself. This takes some skill and a dash of confidence, but when the dough is properly folded and shaped, it bakes into a heavenly light structure with a crust that shatters when cut with a knife.

Active dry yeast	1½ teaspoons
Table salt	2 teaspoons
Warm water	1.75 ounces
Unbleached bread flour	16 ounces
Cool water	13 ounces
Vegetable oil	

What's New

- Ciabatta has the most water of any dough in this book.
- Ciabatta dough is looser in structure and texture than focaccia dough.
- The ciabatta bakes darker than the baguette or focaccia.

MEASURE AND WEIGH Measure the yeast and the salt separately and set them aside.

Weigh the warm water into a small bowl. The warm water should feel hot to the touch, between 105° and 115°F. Sprinkle the yeast on top of the water, stir to dissolve, and set aside.

Weigh the flour into a large mixing bowl. Sprinkle the salt on top of the flour, stir to incorporate, and then make a well in the center.

Weigh the cool water into a small bowl. The cool water temperature should be between 70° and 75°F. Refer to page 17 to calculate the exact temperature and measure it with a thermometer, or gauge the approximate temperature by touch.

MIX Add the yeast mixture to the flour, stir 3 or 4 turns, then, little by little, add the cool water. Mix with your hands for 2 to 3 minutes, until all of the ingredients are incorporated, the grit of the salt is dissolved, and the dough forms a rough and shaggy mass, and then stop.

LET THE DOUGH REST Cover the bowl with a kitchen towel or plastic wrap and let the dough stand still for about 30 minutes.

FOLD Sprinkle your work surface with flour and then use a plastic bowl scraper to scrape the dough out onto it. Tap your hands in a little flour, then gently flatten the dough into a rectangle, with the short side facing you.

Use your fingers or the plastic scraper to flip the top edge of the dough down to just below the center, then flip the bottom edge up to just above the center. Repeat this process for the right and left sides, then turn the dough over and dust off the flour.

This wet dough will benefit from a second fold; let the dough relax for 1 to 2 minutes after the first fold, then sprinkle a little more flour on your work surface and fold a second time.

FERMENT Oil a second large bowl, then place the dough in it, seam side up, to oil the top. Then turn it seam side down, and cover the bowl with oiled plastic wrap. Mark the time with a felt-tipped pen on the plastic wrap and allow the dough to rest and rise in a moderately cool place until the dough has doubled in volume, 1 to 2 hours, depending on the heat of your environment.

After the first 30 minutes of fermentation, turn the dough out of the bowl onto your work surface, and fold again as described above. Return the dough to the bowl, cover, and complete the fermentation.

The dough is folded again to build strength, which is necessary because this is a highly hydrated dough.

CUT AND SHAPE Once the dough has doubled in volume, sprinkle a lot of flour onto your work surface, and prepare a proofing place for the ciabatta by sprinkling the same amount of flour onto the back of an inverted baking sheet.

Use the plastic scraper to scrape the dough out onto the work surface, letting it assume its natural shape. Tap your hands in flour, and gently flatten the dough into a large, even rectangle measuring approximately 12 by 8 inches and 1 inch thick.

Use a metal bench scraper or knife to cut the dough into 4 equal pieces, approximately 4 by 6 inches. Gently place them on the floured back of the baking sheet.

PROOF Cover the ciabatta with oiled plastic wrap and let proof until the dough has doubled in volume, 30 to 45 minutes.

While the shaped dough is proofing, preheat the oven to 480°F, with an empty pan for creating steam on the bottom of the oven. Have ready a spritzer filled with water near the oven and approximately 8 ounces of hot water to pour into the empty pan.

Once the dough has approximately doubled in volume, sprinkle more flour on the work surface. Take 1 dough piece at a time and stretch it very gently to lengthen it by 2 to 3 inches, then place it on the floured area of your counter. Dust off your baking sheet, turn it right side up and oil it, and place each piece upside down on the baking sheet.

BAKE Open the oven door, and, working quickly, slide the baking sheet with the ciabatta onto the middle rack, then pour the hot water into the empty pan below to create steam before quickly closing the oven door. After 1 minute, open the oven door and spritz around the dough with water, then close the door again.

The ciabatta should bake to a very dark brown in 45 to 55 minutes.

⫸ As the pieces of ciabatta proof on the floured surface, they pick up a pattern of flour that will show with beautiful striations once the loaves are turned over to bake.

⫸ Both stretching the ciabatta and turning the dough upside down elongate and open up air pockets in the dough.

COOL Let the ciabatta cool completely on a wire rack. After the bread has cooled, use a serrated knife to cut it horizontally through the center, and take a look at the interior.

Ideally you will have baked the ciabatta to a very dark brown so that the caramelization of the crust permeates the entire flavor of the bread, and the crust is eggshell thin, perfect for a sandwich. The holes in the crumb will be large, embedded in the cobweb strands of glistening dough; notice how much lighter the ciabatta is than the focaccia, and how much larger the holes of the crumb are.

THESE THREE DOUGHS MAKE CLASSIC SHAPES

As you will begin to understand, both altering the water quantity and changing the shape of the dough suddenly increase your repertoire of breads by a hundredfold—one of the secrets by which a baker lives. The new shapes in this chapter—especially the boule and the batard—and the baguette from the previous chapter are versatile forms to work from. These shapes, and those spawned from them, will also begin to appear in subsequent chapters of this book. In addition, you may want to vary some of the recipes that come later in this book by forming them into the shapes of your choosing. Once your hands are practiced in these techniques, you can be creative and add a little pizzazz.

⋙ Practice your skills by using the baguette dough on page 35 to shape boules and batards.

⋙ Before shaping any dough, prepare your work space so that it's free and clear, especially from any small knots or clumps of dough, and make sure it's properly floured with a light dusting thrown evenly across your counter.

FOLDING

Folding a dough lines up the gluten into structured sheets and builds up a little strength. Sprinkle your work surface with flour and scrape the dough out onto it. Tap your hands in a little flour, then gently flatten the dough into a rectangle, with the short side facing you **(A)**. Use your fingers or a plastic scraper to flip the top edge of the dough down to just below the center **(B, C, D)**, then flip the bottom edge up to just above the center **(E, F)**. Repeat this process for the right **(G, H)** and left sides **(I, J)**, then turn the dough over and dust off the flour **(K, L)**.

Folding

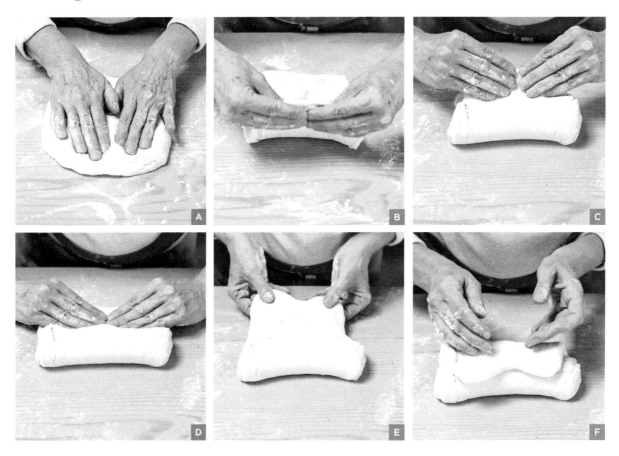

Folding (continued)

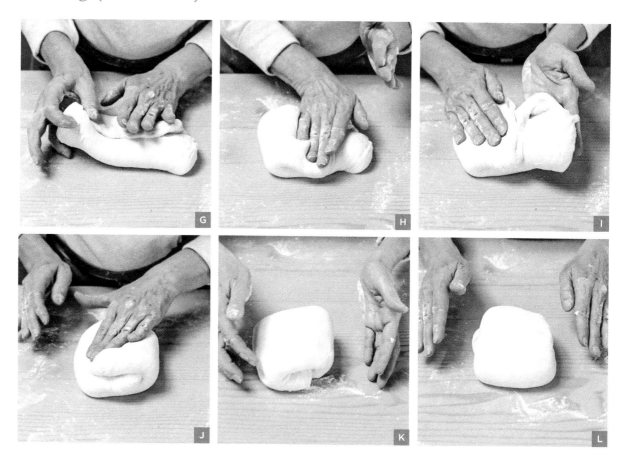

SHAPING A FILONE

A filone is a fatter, wider, and stubbier version of the baguette. Begin with a pre-shaped log (see page 7), with the long side of the rectangle facing you. After the log has rested for 10 minutes, fold the dough in half lengthwise, and then in half again so that the width is 3 to 4 inches, then complete the pull, tuck, and seal as if making a baguette (see page 37), and stop. The dough should be looser in structure than the baguette.

SHAPING A BATARD

➤ The batard shape is also the starting point for the shape to be used for a pan loaf.

Begin with a pre-shaped log (see page 7) placed lengthwise in front of you with the seam side up. Fold the dough in half lengthwise and press down so that it adheres to itself **(A)**. Close the interior gap by pulling dough from the top with your left hand and sealing at the bottom with the heel of your right hand, as you would for a baguette **(B)**. Place the dough seam-side down, then place your hands at the center, fingers together, and with gentle but consistent pressure move your hands away from each other, rolling back and forth toward the ends of the dough.

Shaping a Batard

CUTTING AN EPI

Making an epi involves using scissors to cut the image of a sheath of wheat from a baguette shape. First, place a shaped and proofed baguette in front of you (see pages 37 to 39 for how to shape a baguette). Hold a pair of scissors horizontally above the dough, not at an angle **(A)**. Gather the dough between the scissor blades, then snip, and pull the snipped piece of dough to the right **(B)**. Repeat snipping again immediately below the first cut, pulling the snipped piece of dough to the left. Continue snipping, pulling right, then left, down the length of the baguette. Because the epi shape is fragile, it is easier to place the baguette on a baking sheet before cutting with scissors, then bake it on the baking sheet.

Cutting an Epi

SHAPING A BOULE

Begin with the dough just scraped out of the bowl and patted into a rectangle (not folded). Pick up one of the edges of dough and pull it toward the center, then gently press it down **(A)**. Repeat pulling and pressing all around the edge of the dough to form a rough circle **(B)**. Make sure all of the pieces of dough adhere to the center **(C)**, then flip the dough over **(D, E)**. In order to seal the dough at the bottom, cup the dough so that there is a sliver of dough between the heels of both hands **(F)**. Move the right hand up and the left hand down, using the table for friction to seal the bottom and to stretch the dough over the top to form a smooth, tight, round structure **(G, H)**. Leave the seam side down on the table **(I)**. Follow the same steps to make a miche, which is a very large boule, or a roll, which is a very small boule.

OTHER SHAPES FOR SOFTER DOUGHS

The shapes that you have just learned about are generally used with stronger doughs, including those made with white flour, whole wheat, or rye. The softer doughs, such as focaccia and ciabatta, can be made into looser batards or boules that will not hold their shape as tightly, but they can also be made into the following shapes:

Focaccia
Breadsticks (page 74)
Fougasse (page 141)

Ciabatta
Rolls (page 80)
Pizza (page 161)
Crackers (page 163)

Shaping a Boule

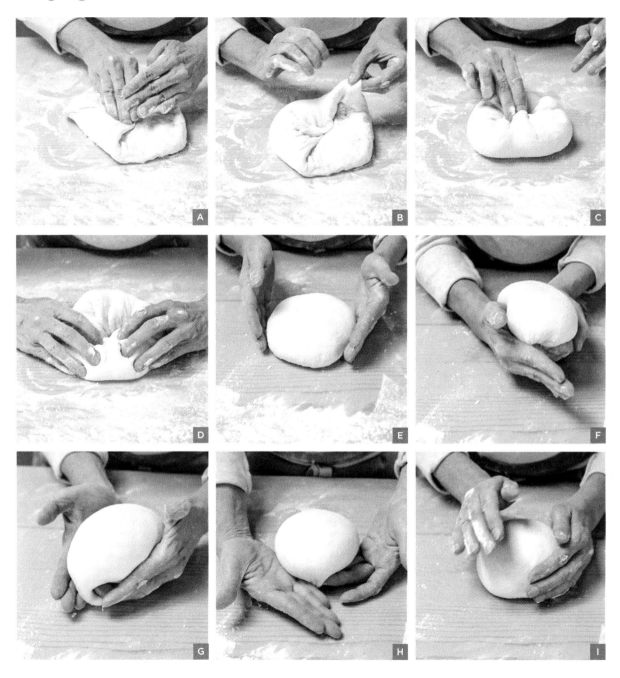

HOW BREADS GOT THEIR NAMES

The names of breads and wordplay surrounding these names are a part of the romance and intrigue of bread making. They bring to mind a host of associations, including the magic of place and the passion of a baker—the kinds of personal experiences that make us think and talk about the very broad categories of "French" or "Italian" bread in a familiar way. Here are some of the more traditional names of breads, their region of development, and their history.

Baguette
From the Latin *baculum*, meaning "stick" or "staff." The baguette was a child of the Industrial Revolution, created by the famous Viennese bakers exploring the possibilities of their new steam-injected ovens. It proved to be less time-consuming and labor-intensive than traditional larger loaves requiring longer fermentations. French bakers quickly adopted the loaf, and the world was delighted—the baguette became the "it" bread of the nineteenth century.

Batard
From the French, meaning "bastard." The batard is the baguette's fall from grace, a "bastardized" version of the baguette. Broader, thicker, and stubbier than its ballerina-esque counterpart, what it lacks in looks it makes up for in practicality—it is more generous in volume, is easier to carry, and holds up in a sandwich.

Boule
French, meaning "ball." *Boule* refers to the shape of the traditional French breads—puffed rustic rounds scored by the village baker. Boules are so traditionally French that the word is the basis for the French term for "baker," *boulanger*, and "bakery," *boulangerie*.

Ciabatta
From the Italian, literally meaning "carpet slipper." Due to its appearance, which is because it's made with a slack dough, the Italians have named this oddly shaped, flat bread after an old shoe—imagine the shapeless slippers the Seven Dwarfs march about in. The ciabatta lends itself to being stuffed with sandwich fixings or grilled into panini. Its crispy, flour-streaked crust encases a soft and tender interior that's looped with irregular holes. It is the ultimate trencher for salads and sauces.

Couronne
French, meaning "crown." This majestic bread shape is achieved by beading balls of bread dough into a ring of rolls that bakes into a splendid, crusty crown.

Epi
From the French, meaning "ear" (as in, ear of wheat). Before baking, rods of baguette dough are snipped into flaps, which when pulled from the oven resemble golden brown ears of wheat. A well-made *pain d'epi* is a true homage to an essential element of bread and life—wheat.

Ficelle
French, meaning "string." Razor thin, the ficelle is the baguette's little string bean of a sister; this bread is for those who savor the crunch and crackle of a good bread crust.

Filone
The Italian word *filone* seems to have several possible translations, including "line," "thread," and "vein," though in truth this bread is a fatter version of the baguette.

Focaccia
From the Latin *panis focacius*, meaning "hearth bread" (*panis* means "bread"; *focus* means "center" or "hearth"). Focaccia is a yeasted Italian flatbread that, in its simplest variation, is dimpled with pockets of olive oil and topped with herbs and coarse salt. Disseminated throughout centuries and cultures, focaccia now exists with a countless variation of names, forms, and flavors. In the south of France, it has surfaced as the stunning leaf-shaped fougasse; in Sicily, it is known as pizza; in northern Italy, it has been mixed with lard for a flaky crumb; and, in northwest Italian regions, you will encounter it topped with raisins, honey, or sugar—*focaccia dolce*.

PART THREE

BUILDING FLAVOR AND TEXTURE

an hour at room temperature first). As the poolish develops, it rises to the top of the bowl in a gentle arc, and the liquid ripens and blooms with lots of luxurious bubbles and with the sweet and sharp aromas from the combination of wheat and acidity. This aromatic quality translates to the finished bread in a nuanced way, perfect for enhancing but not overwhelming the flavor of a baguette or similar bread. Due to the fragile liquid nature of this preferment, after 12 hours the volume will collapse and the pronounced acidity will be harmful to a healthy dough development.

Biga means "starter" in Italian, and like a poolish, it contains no salt, but it is a much stiffer preferment for the practical purpose of enduring a longer fermentation in order to add more acidic flavor development to the bread. To manage its pronounced acidity, the biga should ferment in a very cool temperature of approximately 40°F, or in the refrigerator, for up to 12 hours.

Note the handling qualities of the baguette, focaccia, and ciabatta doughs made with preferments compared to the same doughs made without preferments. The body of the dough should feel voluptuous, and the quality of the dough should be a little silkier and smoother. There will be a noticeable sheen, and the extensibility will be improved—feel how much easier it is to roll a baguette and to stretch the ciabatta. Finally, both the flavor and the texture of a bread made with a preferment will be invigorated with a more robust quality of crumb and crust.

As we develop flavor and add fortification to the structure of the dough, we can begin to evolve the shapes, both for variety and to practice the skills required to take your bread to the next level. The baguette dough turns into the vulnerable and graceful epi; the focaccia is stretched wide and thin into stellar flat breadsticks; the ciabatta is hand-cut into rolls that are ethereal and light.

Epis and Ficelles
(Baguette Dough with Poolish)

AN EPI IS A GRACEFUL AND EASY WAY to change up the baguette to a more festive presentation. The epi can be shared around the dinner table and broken apart by hand, each leaf-shape roll showing off the rich flavor from the poolish. A ficelle is simply a skinnier version of the baguette, but it makes a perfect sandwich bread, sliced open and stuffed with cheeses and salami or roasted vegetables.

YIELD
28 to 30 ounces dough;
3 small epis or 6 or 7 ficelles, each
12 to 14 inches long

POOLISH (MAKES 8 OUNCES)

Active dry yeast	½ teaspoon
Warm water	4 ounces
Unbleached bread flour	4 ounces

EPIS OR FICELLES

Active dry yeast	1 teaspoon
Table salt	2 teaspoons
Warm water	1.75 ounces
Unbleached bread flour	12 ounces
Cool water	6 ounces
Poolish (above)	8 ounces
Vegetable oil	

>>> Remember, a poolish needs time to ferment before you can proceed with the dough. Let's say you want to serve your epis with dinner, following the sample schedule on page 34. To make your epis with a poolish, you can either make it early in the morning, so that your poolish can ferment until noon, or you can make it the night before, and let it cold-ferment in your refrigerator until the next day. Due to the fragile nature of this preferment, it should not be held for more than 12 hours in the refrigerator; you can take it out of the refrigerator 30 to 60 minutes before you plan to use it.

Poolish

MEASURE AND WEIGH Measure the yeast and set it aside.

Weigh the warm water into a small bowl. The warm water should feel hot to the touch, between 105° and 115°F. Sprinkle the yeast on top of the water, stir to dissolve, and set aside.

Weigh the flour into a medium mixing bowl and then make a well in the center.

MIX Add the yeast mixture to the flour. Stir 3 or 4 turns, until all of the ingredients are incorporated.

FERMENT Cover the bowl with plastic wrap and allow to ferment at room temperature for 3 to 4 hours, or refrigerated for 12 hours.

⋙ After 1 to 2 hours at room temperature, the poolish can be put into the refrigerator to finish developing for up to 12 hours.

Epis or Ficelles

MEASURE AND WEIGH Measure the yeast and the salt separately and set them aside.

Weigh the warm water into a small bowl. The warm water should feel hot to the touch, between 105° and 115°F. Sprinkle the yeast on top of the water, stir to dissolve, and set aside.

Weigh the flour into a large mixing bowl. (Remember that the poolish has 4 ounces of the flour quantity from our original foundation dough, so the amount of flour here has been decreased to 12 ounces.) Sprinkle the salt on top of the flour, stir to incorporate, and then make a well in the center.

Weigh the cool water into a small bowl. (Remember that the poolish has 4 ounces of the water quantity from our original foundation dough, so the amount of cool water here has been decreased to 6 ounces.)

MIX First, combine the poolish with the cool water, using your fingers to help break up the pieces so that they begin to dissolve in the water. Add the yeast mixture to the flour, stir 3 or 4 turns, and then, little by little, add the cool water with the poolish. Mix with your hands for

⋙ To find the accurate water temperature, you will need to factor in the poolish, so multiply: 75 x 4 (because the poolish counts as the fourth factor) = 300. Now subtract the room temperature, flour temperature, poolish temperature, and friction factor (see page 17) to get the appropriate water temperature for your dough. If the poolish is cool (if it has been held in the refrigerator), the necessary water temperature will be warmer, probably between 75° and 85°F.

2 to 3 minutes, until all of the ingredients are incorporated, the grit of the salt is dissolved, and the dough forms a rough and shaggy mass, and then stop.

LET THE DOUGH REST Cover the bowl with a kitchen towel or plastic wrap and let the dough stand still for about 30 minutes.

FOLD Sprinkle your work surface with flour and then use a plastic bowl scraper to scrape the dough out onto it. Tap your hands in a little flour, then gently flatten the dough into a rectangle, with the short side facing you.

Use your fingers or the plastic scraper to flip the top edge of the dough down to just below the center, then flip the bottom edge up to just above the center. Repeat this process for the right and left sides, then turn the dough over and dust off the flour.

FERMENT Oil a second large bowl, then place the dough in it, seam side up, to oil the top. Then turn it seam side down, and cover the bowl with oiled plastic wrap. Mark the time with a felt-tipped pen on the plastic wrap and allow the dough to rest and rise in a moderately cool place until it has doubled in volume, 1 to 2 hours, depending on the heat of your environment.

CUT, PRE-SHAPE, REST, AND SHAPE Once the dough has doubled in volume, sprinkle a little more flour onto your work surface, then scrape the dough out onto it and let the dough assume its natural shape. Dust the top of the dough with a little flour and pat it down gently, then divide it into 3 pieces of 8 to 9 ounces each for the epis, or 6 or 7 pieces of about 4 ounces each for the ficelles; or make a few of each to shape and bake at the same time.

Let all of the pieces of dough rest for 5 minutes, covered with oiled plastic wrap.

Pre-shape the dough into logs, following the instructions on page 7. Cover the logs with oiled plastic wrap and let rest for 5 to 10 minutes.

≫ Mixing this dough will feel a little different, as the water with the poolish will require a few more hand strokes to completely incorporate all of the ingredients. After about 2 minutes of mixing, the dough should appear rough and shaggy.

≫ If you are planning to make the breadstick recipe on page 74, you may use a portion of this dough as the pâte fermentée. Remove 4 ounces of the dough, place it in a lightly oiled bowl, cover with oiled plastic wrap, and refrigerate for 8 hours or until the following day. You will then end up with slightly smaller epis or one fewer ficelle.

≫ With the addition of the poolish, note how much more extensible the dough is while shaping.

Once the rest period is over, shape the logs: For epis, shape the logs into baguettes, following the instructions on pages 37 to 39. For ficelles, follow the same instructions as for baguettes, but making a skinnier version.

PROOF Follow the instructions on page 39 for couching the baguettes or ficelles. Cover the baguettes or ficelles with oiled plastic wrap and let them proof until doubled in volume, 30 to 45 minutes. Because the poolish gives the dough an extra kick of fermentation, the proof time may be a little shorter than the proof time for baguettes without a preferment. In addition, because ficelles are smaller, they will proof slightly faster than baguettes.

While the shaped dough is proofing, preheat the oven to 480°F, with an empty pan for creating steam on the bottom of the oven. Have ready a spritzer filled with water near the oven and approximately 8 ounces of hot water to pour into the empty pan.

SCORE If you are making ficelles, once they have approximately doubled in volume, dust a little flour on top for a decorative look and smooth the flour gently with your hand, then dip a lame or straight-edge razor in water, and score each ficelle with several horizontal cuts down the center, cutting approximately ½ inch deep. Do not score the baguette logs for epis.

To finish shaping the epis, transfer the baguettes to 1 or 2 oiled baking sheets. Cut into epis with scissors, following the instructions on page 59. If you are making ficelles, transfer them to another oiled baking sheet.

BAKE Open the oven door, and working quickly, slide the baking sheets into the oven. If you are making both epis and ficelles, bake the ficelles on the middle rack and the epis on the rack above. Pour the hot water into the empty pan below to create steam before quickly closing the oven door. After 1 minute, open the oven door, spritz around the dough pieces, then close the door.

If you choose to make both epis and ficelles, they can be baked at the same time, with the epis on the rack above the ficelles; or the epis, uncut (still in their baguette shape), can be moved to the refrigerator halfway through proofing and held until the ficelles are finished baking. If the epis are held back, let them finish proofing before cutting the epi shape.

The ficelles should bake in 20 to 25 minutes, and the epis in 30 to 35 minutes.

COOL Let the ficelles or epis cool completely on a wire rack. After the bread has cooled, use a sharp knife to cut through the center horizontally, and take a look at the interior.

Compare the look and flavor to the baguettes you made on page 35. The color of the crust and the crumb will be a bit richer, and the interior will have a more developed network of holes, probably a little larger than the hole structure within your first baguette. The flavor will be stronger, as the poolish helps to tease out the taste of the wheat in the flour and also adds a bit of acidity.

OTHER SHAPES TO TRY

You could also choose to make 3 or 4 baguettes, following the shaping instructions on pages 37 to 39. Proof, score, and bake as directed on pages 39 to 40.

Focaccia Breadsticks
(with Pâte Fermentée)

YIELD
28 to 30 ounces dough;
12 to 14 breadsticks,
each 12 to 14 inches long

MAKING BREADSTICKS WITH THIS PREFERMENT allows the dough to be stretched easily but also adds a pop of flavor; they are good to go with only olive oil and salt, but they are also very accommodating for any kind of topping, such as olive paste to Parmesan cheese to seeds or dried herbs. After adding the olive oil, spread the olive paste with a spoon or a pastry brush, liberally scatter cheese on top, or sprinkle with seeds or herbs.

✽ You can either make the pâte fermentée new, using the recipe given here, or pull it from a previous dough. The pâte fermentée must be a white dough, such as the baguette dough on page 35, and fully fermented.

PÂTE FERMENTÉE (MAKES 4 OUNCES)

Active dry yeast	¾ teaspoon
Table salt	1½ teaspoons
Warm water	0.5 ounce
Unbleached bread flour	2.5 ounces
Cool water	1 ounce
Vegetable oil	

FOCACCIA BREADSTICKS

Active dry yeast	1 teaspoon
Table salt	1 teaspoon
Warm water	1.75 ounces
Unbleached bread flour	14 ounces
Cool water	10 ounces
Pâte fermentée (above)	4 ounces
Olive oil	2 to 4 tablespoons
Coarse salt	2 teaspoons
Seeds or dried herbs for topping, such as sesame, caraway, rosemary, or a combination (optional)	1 tablespoon

Pâte Fermentée

MEASURE AND WEIGH Measure the yeast and the salt separately and set them aside.

Weigh the warm water into a small bowl. The warm water should feel hot to the touch, between 105° and 115°F. Sprinkle the yeast on top of the water, stir to dissolve, and set aside.

Weigh the flour into a medium mixing bowl. Sprinkle the salt on top of the flour, stir to incorporate, and then make a well in the center.

Weigh the cool water into a small bowl.

MIX Add the yeast mixture to the flour, then the cool water, and stir until all of the ingredients are incorporated, the grit of the salt is dissolved, and the pâte fermentée forms a rough and shaggy mass.

FERMENT Cover the bowl with oiled plastic wrap and mark the time with a felt-tipped pen on the plastic wrap. Allow the pâte fermentée to rest and rise in a moderately cool place until it has doubled in volume, 1 to 2 hours, depending on the heat of your environment.

Focaccia Breadsticks

MEASURE AND WEIGH Measure the yeast and the table salt separately and set them aside. (As there is already salt in the pâte fermentée, the amount of salt here has been reduced to only 1 teaspoon.)

Weigh the warm water into a small bowl. The warm water should feel hot to the touch, between 105° and 115°F. Sprinkle the yeast on top of the water, stir to dissolve, and set aside.

Weigh the flour into a large mixing bowl. Sprinkle the table salt on top of the flour, stir to incorporate, and then make a well in the center.

Weigh the cool water into a small bowl. The cool water temperature should be between 70° and 75°F. (If the pâte fermentée is cold, the necessary water temperature should be higher, probably between 75° and 85°F.)

Depending on your schedule, the pâte fermentée can be placed in the refrigerator after 45 minutes to complete fermentation. It can be held, refrigerated, for 12 hours before you need to proceed with the recipe.

MIX First, combine the pâte fermentée with the cool water, using your fingers to help break up the pieces so that they begin to dissolve in the water. Add the yeast mixture to the flour, stir 3 or 4 turns, and then, little by little, add the cool water with the pâte fermentée. Mix with your hands for 2 to 3 minutes, until all of the ingredients are incorporated, the grit of the salt is dissolved, and the dough forms a rough and shaggy mass, and then stop.

LET THE DOUGH REST Cover the bowl with a kitchen towel or plastic wrap and let the dough stand still for about 30 minutes.

FOLD Sprinkle your work surface with flour and then use a plastic bowl scraper to scrape the dough out onto it. Tap your hands in a little flour, then gently flatten the dough into a rectangle, with the short side facing you.

Use your fingers or the plastic scraper to flip the top edge of the dough down to just below the center, then flip the bottom edge up to just above the center. Repeat this process for the right and left sides, then turn the dough over and dust off the flour.

FERMENT Oil a second large bowl, then place the dough in it, seam side up, to oil the top. Then turn it seam side down, and cover the bowl with oiled plastic wrap. Mark the time with a felt-tipped pen on the plastic wrap and allow the dough to rest and rise in a moderately cool place until it has doubled in volume, 1 to 2 hours, depending on the heat of your environment.

CUT, PRE-SHAPE, REST, AND SHAPE Once the dough has doubled in volume, sprinkle a little more flour onto your work surface, then scrape the dough out onto it and let the dough assume its natural shape. Dust the top of the dough with a little flour and pat it down gently, then use a metal bench scraper to divide it into twelve to fourteen 2-ounce pieces.

Gently pull each piece to elongate it and place on an oiled baking sheet, then cover with oiled plastic wrap and let rest for 10 to 15 minutes.

Mixing this dough will feel a little different, and it will require a few more hand strokes to completely incorporate the water with the pâte fermentée into the other ingredients.

When the dough has finished resting, take each piece between your hands and pull, then stretch, all the while gently shaking, until the dough stretches to the length of your baking sheet. The dough should stretch fairly easily and be about 1 inch wide, with slightly pointy ends. As you finish, set each breadstick back on the oiled baking sheet.

PROOF Cover the breadsticks with oiled plastic wrap and let proof until the dough has doubled in volume, 20 to 30 minutes.

While the shaped dough is proofing, preheat the oven to 480°F, with a rack in the middle of the oven for baking and an empty pan for creating steam on the bottom of the oven. Have ready a spritzer filled with water near the oven and approximately 8 ounces of hot water to pour into the empty pan.

BAKE If the dough has contracted after proofing, stretch the breadsticks back into shape. Use a pastry brush to pat the dough with the olive oil, dimple it very gently with your fingers, and sprinkle the breadsticks with the coarse salt and seeds or herbs, if using. Open the oven door and, working quickly, slide the baking sheet with the breadsticks into the oven and pour the hot water into the empty pan below to create steam before quickly closing the oven door. After 1 minute, open the oven door, spritz around the breadsticks with water, then close the door.

The breadsticks should bake to a golden brown in 25 to 30 minutes.

COOL Let the breadsticks cool completely on a wire rack.

When the breadsticks have cooled, snap one in half to hear how crispy it sounds. The extra flavor development from the pâte fermentée should make these breadsticks addictively delicious and fun to eat— they will be the hit of your party.

⧉ You should be able to fit all of the breadsticks on 1 baking sheet, but you might want to have a second baking sheet ready in case you need the extra space, especially if your breadsticks are fatter.

OTHER SHAPES TO TRY

This dough can be baked as one large sheet of focaccia, with the toppings of your choice. Press and dimple the dough onto a rimmed baking sheet, proof, and bake as directed on pages 45 to 46. This dough can also be shaped into small rolls of 2 to 3 ounces each, shaped as directed on pages 60 to 61, and topped with olive oil and salt or the toppings listed above. For proofing and baking times, follow the instructions for the ciabatta rolls on pages 84 to 85.

Ciabatta Rolls
(with Biga)

YIELD
28 to 30 ounces dough;
12 to 14 small oval rolls

BECAUSE THE DOUGH in this recipe has a minimum amount of handling, these crisp and tender little breads—cut into dainty rolls using a biscuit cutter—are amazingly light and airy, with webs of glistening dough surrounding a network of large and small holes, all captured by a thin and crisp crust.

BIGA (MAKES 10 OUNCES)

Active dry yeast	½ teaspoon
Warm water	4 ounces
Unbleached bread flour	6 ounces

CIABATTA ROLLS

Active dry yeast	1 teaspoon
Table salt	2 teaspoons
Warm water	1.75 ounces
Unbleached bread flour	10 ounces
Cool water	8 ounces
Biga (above)	10 ounces
Vegetable oil	

BIGA

MEASURE AND WEIGH Measure the yeast and set it aside.

Weigh the warm water into a small bowl. The warm water should feel hot to the touch, between 105° and 115°F. Sprinkle the yeast on top of the water, stir to dissolve, and set aside.

Weigh the flour into a large mixing bowl and then make a well in the center.

MIX Add the yeast mixture to the flour and stir until all of the ingredients are incorporated.

FERMENT Cover the bowl with plastic wrap and allow to ferment in the refrigerator for at least 8 hours, or up to 12 hours.

Ciabatta Rolls

MEASURE AND WEIGH Measure the yeast and the salt separately and set them aside.

Weigh the warm water into a small bowl. The warm water should feel hot to the touch, between 105° and 115°F. Sprinkle the yeast on top of the water, stir to dissolve, and set aside.

Weigh the flour into a large mixing bowl. Sprinkle the salt on top of the flour, stir to incorporate, and then make a well in the center.

Weigh the cool water into a small bowl. Since the biga will be cold, the water temperature should be higher than for other breads, between 75° and 85°F.

MIX First, combine the biga with the cool water, using your fingers to help break up the pieces so that they begin to dissolve in the water. Add the yeast mixture to the flour, stir 3 or 4 turns, and then, little by little, add the cool water with the biga. Mix with your hands for 2 to 3 minutes, until all of the ingredients are incorporated, the grit of the salt is dissolved, and the dough forms a rough and shaggy mass, and then stop.

LET THE DOUGH REST Cover the bowl with a kitchen towel or plastic wrap and let the dough stand still for about 30 minutes.

FOLD Sprinkle your work surface with flour and then use a plastic bowl scraper to scrape the dough out onto it. Tap your hands in a little flour, then gently flatten the dough into a rectangle, with the short side facing you.

>≫ Because this is a stiffer preferment, it will require more stirring.

>≫ As you mix, it will take a little more work to break down the biga in the water, though the total amount of water in this wet dough lets you truly feel the strands of gluten as they stretch and break and then re-form into a watery mass.

Use your fingers or the plastic scraper to flip the top edge of the dough down to just below the center, then flip the bottom edge up to just above the center. Repeat this process for the right and left sides, then turn the dough over and dust off the flour.

FERMENT Oil a second large bowl, then place the dough in it, seam side up, to oil the top. Then turn it seam side down, and cover the bowl with oiled plastic wrap. Mark the time with a felt-tipped pen on the plastic wrap and allow the dough to rest and rise in a moderately cool place until it has doubled in volume, 1 to 2 hours, depending on the heat of your environment.

CUT Toward the end of the fermentation time, prepare a proofing place for the ciabatta by sprinkling a lot of flour on the back of an inverted baking sheet.

Once the dough has doubled in volume, sprinkle a little more flour onto your work surface, then scrape the dough out onto it and let the dough assume its natural shape. Dust the top of the dough with a little flour and pat it down gently, then tap your hands in flour, and gently flatten the dough into a large, even rectangle. If necessary, slip your hands under the dough to pull and stretch it to an even thickness of 1 to 2 inches.

Dip a 3-inch round biscuit cutter into a little flour, then use it to cut the dough into 12 to 14 pieces, pressing with full strength into the dough. Pull each cut piece away, place it on the back of the floured baking sheet, and cover with oiled plastic wrap as you continue to cut the remaining pieces.

PROOF Let the rolls proof, covered with oiled plastic wrap, until the dough has doubled in volume, 20 to 30 minutes. Because you have not strengthened the dough by vigorously shaping it, the rolls will proof a little more quickly than your first ciabatta recipe on page 50.

While the dough is proofing, preheat the oven to 480°F, with an empty pan for creating steam on the bottom of the oven. Have ready a spritzer filled with water near the oven and approximately 8 ounces of hot water to pour into the empty pan.

Although you can use your metal bench scraper to cut rolls, a biscuit cutter makes a uniquely elegant little roll, and the shape actually contributes to the open network of holes in the crumb. If desired, you can keep the extra dough scraps to use as a preferment for another bread the next day.

Once the rolls have approximately doubled in volume, oil a second baking sheet. Take 1 piece of dough at a time and stretch it very gently to lengthen it into a 4-by-2-inch oval shape. This is the only shaping to be done. Place each piece of dough upside down on the oiled baking sheet.

BAKE After all of the rolls have been stretched into shape and placed on the baking sheet, open the oven door, and, working quickly, slide the baking sheet with the rolls onto the middle rack, then pour the hot water into the empty pan below to create steam before quickly closing the oven door.

The rolls should bake to a very dark brown in 25 to 35 minutes.

COOL Let the rolls cool completely on a wire rack. After the rolls have cooled, use a sharp knife to cut through the center of 1 roll horizontally, and take a look at the interior of this bread.

≫ Both stretching the dough and turning it upside down affect the interior crumb, making a larger network of holes and contributing to the airiness of the baked bread.

OTHER SHAPES TO TRY

You could also shape this dough into four rectangular ciabatta loaves. Shape, proof, and bake as directed on page 52.

TEASING OUT THE FLAVORS OF DIFFERENT GRAINS

With a broadened sense of how to develop flavor and texture using white flour and preferments in breads, we can apply this knowledge to whole wheat, rye, and semolina flours, using different ingredients and methods to bring out the specific flavors from these grains.

The three bread recipes in this chapter follow European history, tradition, and the terroir of France, Germany, and Italy. We will make a big French whole wheat miche, a German rye, and an Italian semolina bread. The characteristics of these breads, which reflect the soil, climate, and culture of their locales, lead to recipes that step beyond the nuanced flavor profiles of white flour and into the realm of hearty tastes, nutrient-rich textures, and bold shapes.

French Whole Wheat Pain de Campagne

YIELD
38 to 40 ounces dough;
1 large miche

BEFORE THE BAGUETTE, there was *pain de campagne*, "bread of the countryside," considered to be the true bread of France. This is a rustic bread that is traditionally made with a combination of white flour and whole wheat or rye, along with a preferment. Nuances of mineral soil, the tang of local yeast, the climate of the year, the strain of wheat (and how it was tended and milled), and the quality of water (hard or soft; rain, river, or well) all tell the story of this bread.

Pain de campagne is usually shaped as a large, round miche, and the large shape comes from the tradition of baking village bread in a communal oven. Back in the day, when baking was only done once a week, both the large size and the preferment served the keeping quality of the bread. In this particular recipe, the preferment, which is also made with whole wheat flour, helps to translate the deeper, richer flavor of the whole wheat flour into the bread.

PÂTE FERMENTÉE (MAKES 10 OUNCES)

Active dry yeast	¾ teaspoon
Table salt	1½ teaspoons
Warm water	2 ounces
Whole wheat flour	6 ounces
Cool water	2 ounces

What's New

* Whole wheat flour is incorporated into the dough.
* A preferment, made with whole wheat flour, is used.
* The dough is shaped into a miche.

Pain de Campagne

Active dry yeast	1 teaspoon
Table salt	1½ teaspoons
Warm water	1.75 ounces
Unbleached bread flour	8 ounces
Whole wheat flour	8 ounces
Cool water	11 ounces
Pâte fermentée (page 87)	10 ounces
Vegetable oil	

Pâte Fermentée

MEASURE AND WEIGH Measure the yeast and the salt separately and set them aside.

Weigh the warm water into a small bowl. The warm water should feel hot to the touch, between 105° and 115°F. Sprinkle the yeast on top of the water, stir to dissolve, and set aside.

Weigh the flour into a medium mixing bowl. Sprinkle the salt on top of the flour, stir to incorporate, and then make a well in the center.

Weigh the cool water into a small bowl.

MIX Add the yeast mixture to the flour, then the cool water, and stir until all of the ingredients are incorporated, the grit of the salt is dissolved, and the pâte fermentée forms a rough and shaggy mass, and then stop.

FERMENT Cover the bowl with oiled plastic wrap and mark the time with a felt-tipped pen on the plastic wrap. Allow the pâte fermentée to rest and rise in a moderately cool place until it has doubled in volume, 1 to 2 hours, depending on the heat of your environment.

Depending on your schedule, the pâte fermentée can be placed in the refrigerator after 45 minutes to complete fermentation. It can be held for 12 hours before you need to proceed with the recipe.

Pain de Campagne

MEASURE AND WEIGH Measure the yeast and the salt separately and set them aside.

Weigh the warm water into a small bowl. The warm water should feel hot to the touch, between 105° and 115°F. Sprinkle the yeast on top of the water, stir to dissolve, and set aside.

Weigh the bread flour and whole wheat flour and combine in a large mixing bowl. Sprinkle the salt on top of the flours, stir to incorporate, and then make a well in the center.

Weigh the cool water into a medium bowl. The cool water temperature should be between 70° and 75°F. (If the pâte fermentée is cold, the necessary water temperature should be higher, probably between 75° and 85°F.)

MIX First, combine the pâte fermentée with the cool water, using your fingers to help break up the pieces so that they begin to dissolve in the water. Add the yeast mixture to the flour, stir 3 or 4 turns, and then, little by little, add the cool water with the pâte fermentée. Mix with your hands for 2 to 3 minutes, until all of the ingredients are incorporated, the grit of the salt is dissolved, and the dough forms a rough and shaggy mass, and then stop.

LET THE DOUGH REST Cover the bowl with a kitchen towel or plastic wrap and let the dough stand still for about 30 minutes.

FOLD Sprinkle your work surface with flour and then use a plastic bowl scraper to scrape the dough out onto it. Tap your hands in a little flour, then gently flatten the dough into a rectangle, with the short side facing you.

Use your fingers or the plastic scraper to flip the top edge of the dough down to just below the center, then flip the bottom edge up to just above the center. Repeat this process for the right and left sides, then turn the dough over and dust off the flour.

While mixing the two flours, feel the difference between the white flour and the whole wheat—there is a grit and a rough coarseness to the whole wheat flour.

This is a stiff dough, and with the addition of whole wheat flour it's going to take some patience and some muscle to incorporate all of the ingredients together. Take your time, stir with your hand from the center to pull the flours to you as the water is added, and bit by bit, the dough will form a mass. If the dough feels too dry, add another ounce or two of water.

FERMENT Oil a second large bowl, then place the dough in it, seam side up, to oil the top. Then turn it seam side down, and cover the bowl with oiled plastic wrap. Mark the time with a felt-tipped pen on the plastic wrap and allow the dough to rest and rise in a moderately cool place until it has doubled in volume, 1 to 2 hours, depending on the heat of your environment.

SHAPE Once the dough has doubled in volume, sprinkle a little more flour onto your work surface, then scrape the dough out onto it and let the dough assume its natural shape. Dust the top of the dough with a little flour and pat it down gently.

Shape the dough into a large round miche, following the instructions for shaping a boule on pages 60 and 61.

PROOF Place a non-textured kitchen towel in a large bowl and coat it heavily with whole wheat flour, then place the miche seam side up on the towel. Cover the miche with oiled plastic wrap and let it proof until the dough has doubled in volume, 45 to 60 minutes.

Because this dough has a long proofing time, wait 30 minutes, then preheat the oven to 480°F, with an empty pan for creating steam on the bottom of the oven. Have ready approximately 16 ounces of hot water to pour into the empty pan.

SCORE Once the miche has doubled in volume, tip it out of the bowl onto an oiled baking sheet. Since the towel for proofing the dough was heavily floured, it may be necessary to gently brush some of the flour from the miche or scrape it off with a metal bench scraper. Dip a lame or straightedge razor in water, and score the dough with decorative cuts as pictured at right.

BAKE Open the oven door, and, working quickly, slide the baking sheet with the miche onto the middle rack of the oven and pour half of the hot water into the empty pan below to create steam before quickly closing the oven door. After 1 minute, open the oven door and pour the rest of the water into the pan, then close the door.

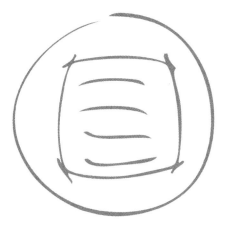

Adding more water to the pan is preferable here to spritzing the dough, since spritzing with water may negatively mark the decorative pattern on top of the miche.

The miche will bake to a very dark brown in 45 to 55 minutes.

COOL Let the miche cool on a wire rack. When the bread has cooled, use a serrated knife to cut the bread in two, and take a look at the interior.

The crumb should be a little sturdier than any of your previous breads, with a smaller network of holes. The rich and earthy aroma of whole wheat and the complex overtones from the acidic development of the preferment should combine to provide a remarkable taste sensation.

OTHER SHAPES TO TRY

You could choose to shape this into four small boules instead of one large miche. If you shape it into four smaller boules, the proofing time will be cut in half (20 to 30 minutes), and these smaller shapes will not require a floured towel in a bowl for a proofing structure. Bake for 30 to 35 minutes on an oiled baking sheet.

German Rye with a Seed and Grain Soaker

SINCE THE MIDDLE AGES, rye has been cultivated in northern and eastern Europe, where the soil and the climate are particularly suitable for this crop. Rye flour is heavier and darker in color compared to wheat flours and is also lower in protein. Lower protein means less gluten, and this noticeably affects the rye dough's ability to ferment with the same extensibility as a wheat flour. For this reason, rye flour produces breads with a much denser structure but with flavors and aromas that can be extraordinarily deep and rich, and these magnificent breads have promoted a notable baking profession in Germany.

This particular recipe combines an array of grains and seeds, each of which has its own flavor profile and health benefits. Since some of the grains included need to be softened for digestibility, we will make a "soaker," and this method of soaking them in water becomes a part of the dough-making procedure.

YIELD
32 to 34 ounces dough;
4 mini batards, each 8 to
10 inches long

SOAKER (MAKES 5 TO 6 OUNCES)

Rye berries	0.5 ounce
Golden flax seeds	0.5 ounce
Sesame seeds	0.5 ounce
Tricolored quinoa, preferably sprouted (store-bought)	0.5 ounce
Amaranth	0.5 ounce
Table salt	2 teaspoons
Water	3 to 4 ounces (or to cover)

What's New

* Rye flour is incorporated into the dough.
* A "soaker" of whole grains and seeds is introduced.
* The dough is folded three times.
* The dough is shaped into batards.
* These batards are couched like baguettes.

≫ It is beneficial to add the salt that would normally be included in the dough recipe (2 teaspoons) to the soaker in order to slow down the enzymatic activity that occurs when these grains and seeds are introduced to water.

German Rye

Active dry yeast	1½ teaspoons
Warm water	1.75 ounces
Unbleached bread flour	4 ounces
Whole wheat flour	4 ounces
Rye flour	8 ounces
Cool water	9 ounces
Soaker (page 93)	5 to 6 ounces
Vegetable oil	

Soaker

MEASURE AND WEIGH Into small prep bowls, weigh the rye berries, flax seeds, sesame seeds, quinoa, and amaranth. Combine the grains and seeds in a small mixing bowl. Measure the salt and add it to the grain and seed mixture. Stir to mix well.

SOAK Heat the water until boiling, and pour over the grains and seeds. Cover the bowl with plastic wrap and allow to soak at room temperature for 3 to 4 hours, or 4 to 8 hours refrigerated (let the water in the soaker come to room temperature before placing the soaker in the refrigerator).

German Rye

MEASURE AND WEIGH Measure the yeast and set it aside.

Weigh the warm water into a small bowl. The warm water should feel hot to the touch, between 105° and 115°F. Sprinkle the yeast on top of the water, stir to dissolve, and set aside.

Weigh the bread flour, whole wheat flour, and rye flour and combine them in a large mixing bowl. (The salt has already been added to the soaker.) Stir to incorporate, and then make a well in the center.

≫≫ If your soaker is cold, take this into account when determining the correct overall water temperature.

Weigh the cool water into a small bowl. The cool water temperature should be between 70° and 75°F. Refer to page 17 to calculate the exact temperature, or gauge the approximate temperature by touch. (Remember that the soaker contains a percentage of the final recipe's water, so the amount of cool water here has been reduced.)

≫≫ You'll notice that the flour seems to take a little longer to absorb the water, and you'll need more muscle to mix this dough—it will feel a bit stickier than your previous doughs.

MIX First, combine the soaker with the cool water, using your fingers to help break it up. Add the yeast mixture to the flour, stir 3 or 4 turns, and then, little by little, add the cool water with the soaker. Mix with your hands for 2 to 3 minutes, until all of the ingredients are incorporated and the dough forms a rough and shaggy mass, and then stop.

LET THE DOUGH REST Cover the bowl with a kitchen towel or plastic wrap and let the dough stand still for about 30 minutes.

FOLD Sprinkle your work surface with flour and then use a plastic bowl scraper to scrape the dough out onto it. Tap your hands in a little flour, then gently flatten the dough into a rectangle, with the short side facing you.

Use your fingers or the plastic bowl scraper to flip the top edge of the dough down to just below the center, then flip the bottom edge up to just above the center. Repeat this process for the right and left sides, then turn the dough over and dust off the flour.

FERMENT Oil a second large bowl, then place the dough in it, seam side up, to oil the top. Then turn it seam side down, and cover the bowl with oiled plastic wrap. Mark the time with a felt-tipped pen on the plastic wrap and allow the dough to rest and rise in a moderately cool place until the dough has doubled in volume, 1 to 2 hours, depending on the heat of your environment.

≫≫ Folding this dough three times, every 30 minutes, helps to develop its strength.

After the first 30 minutes of fermentation, turn the dough out of the bowl onto your work surface, and fold a second time as described previously. Then, after 30 more minutes, fold again a third time. Return the dough to the bowl, cover, and complete the fermentation.

CUT, PRE-SHAPE, REST, AND SHAPE Once the dough has doubled in volume, sprinkle a little more flour onto your work surface, then scrape the dough out onto it and let the dough assume its natural shape. Dust the top of the dough with a little flour and pat it down gently. Divide the dough into 4 equal pieces.

Pre-shape each into a log as described on page 7, then cover with oiled plastic wrap and let rest for about 10 minutes before you continue shaping. Shape the logs into batards, following the instructions on page 58.

PROOF To proof the mini batards, take a kitchen towel about the size of your baking sheet, and place it on top of the baking sheet. Tuck the left edge of the towel under itself, then sprinkle the entire towel heavily with flour. Place the first batard, seam side down, on top of the towel at the very upper left end and the second batard below the first. Pull the towel on the right toward the batard to form a loop up against the dough. Place the third and fourth batards on the towel next to the first two, then pull the towel to make another loop. Finish by tucking the right-hand edge of the towel under itself. Cover with oiled plastic wrap and let the batards proof until the dough has doubled in volume, 30 to 40 minutes.

While the shaped dough is proofing, preheat the oven to 480°F, with an empty pan for creating steam on the bottom of the oven. Have ready a spritzer filled with water near the oven and approximately 8 ounces of hot water to pour into the empty pan.

SCORE Once the batards have approximately doubled in volume, transfer them from the towel to an oiled baking sheet. Dust a little flour on top for a decorative look and smooth the flour gently with your hand. Dip a lame or straightedge razor in water, and score each batard as pictured at right, leaving ¼ inch at either end and cutting approximately ½ inch deep.

BAKE Open the oven door, and, working quickly, slide the baking sheet with the batards onto the middle rack, and pour the hot water into the empty pan below to create steam before quickly closing the oven door. After 1 minute, open the oven door, spritz around the dough pieces, then close the door.

The batards should bake in 30 to 35 minutes.

COOL Let the batards cool completely on a wire rack. After the bread has cooled, use a sharp knife to cut through the center horizontally, and take a look at the interior.

Note that the structure of the dough is denser than your previous whole wheat bread (page 87); the soaker will have improved the moisture content and added a lively texture. Most important, the flavor will be unique to these flours and grains. It may take 24 hours of staling, which is the moisture releasing and the bread settling as it cools, before the flavors of this bread make themselves known in a rich, robust, and deeply satisfying way.

OTHER SHAPES TO TRY

You could shape this dough into two large batards or two large boules of 14 to 15 ounces each instead of four small batards; let the larger sizes proof for 35 to 40 minutes (couche the larger batards in the same manner as the small ones), and bake for 40 to 45 minutes.

Italian Semolina Bread with Sweet Butter

THE WORD *SEMOLINA*, which comes from the Latin *simila*, meaning "flour," immediately brings to mind Italian food and bread. Semolina is the coarse pieces that remain after the milling of durum flour, and is used predominantly for making pasta. For a bread called *semolina*, you will use a "patent" durum flour, which is the purest and highest-quality commercial wheat flour available.

The sweet butter in this recipe, which tenderizes the dough, pulls a uniquely rich flavor from the semolina grain and makes for a lovely, delicate crumb.

This dough, often shaped into a filone, can be coated with sesame seeds as it is here, which, when toasted during the bake, pair nicely with the texture of the bread, adding extra flavor and crunch. Of course, sesame seeds are optional, but they meld together with this particular bread as a perfect companion.

YIELD
30 to 32 ounces dough;
2 filones, each 12 to 14 inches long

Unsalted butter	2 ounces
Active dry yeast	1½ teaspoons
Table salt	2 teaspoons
Warm water	1.75 ounces
Unbleached bread flour	8 ounces
Durum flour	8 ounces
Cool water	11 ounces
Sesame seeds	2 tablespoons, or enough for sprinkling on top

What's New

- Patent durum flour, a kind of semolina, is incorporated into the dough.
- Butter is incorporated into the dough.
- The dough is shaped into filones.
- The dough is topped with seeds before baking.

MEASURE AND WEIGH Measure or weigh the butter and put it in the freezer for 15 to 20 minutes.

Measure the yeast and the salt separately and set them aside.

Weigh the warm water into a small bowl. The warm water should feel hot to the touch, between 105° and 115°F. Sprinkle the yeast on top of the water, stir to dissolve, and set aside.

Weigh the bread flour and durum flour and combine in a large mixing bowl. Sprinkle the salt on top of the flour, and stir to incorporate.

Take the butter from the freezer, and, holding it by the wrapper (or parchment paper or plastic wrap) on one end, grate it over the flour mixture using the medium holes of a grater, working until all the butter is in the bowl. (You made need to cut the last remaining piece with a knife to avoid grating your fingers.) With your fingers, working quickly, rub and blend the butter into the flour, then make a well in the center.

Weigh the cool water into a small bowl. The cool water temperature should be between 70° and 75°F. Refer to page 17 to calculate the exact temperature and measure it with a thermometer, or gauge the approximate temperature by touch.

MIX Add the yeast mixture to the flour, stir 3 or 4 turns, and then, little by little, add the cool water. Mix with your hands for 2 to 3 minutes, until all of the ingredients are incorporated, the grit of the salt is dissolved, and the dough forms a mass, and then stop.

LET THE DOUGH REST Cover the bowl with a kitchen towel or plastic wrap and let the dough stand still for about 30 minutes.

FOLD Sprinkle your work surface with flour and then use a plastic bowl scraper to scrape the dough out onto it. Tap your hands in a little flour, then gently flatten the dough into a rectangle, with the short side facing you.

With the added butter, this dough will feel a little slippery while mixing, and it will take a few more hand strokes to completely incorporate all the ingredients. Look for the dough to eventually feel silky and luxurious due to the butter, and check the water absorption of the flour mixture. If the dough is too dry, add another ounce or two of water.

Use your fingers or the plastic scraper to flip the top edge of the dough down to just below the center, then flip the bottom edge up to just above the center. Repeat this process for the right and left sides, then turn the dough over and dust off the flour.

FERMENT Oil a second large bowl, then place the dough in it, seam side up, to oil the top. Then turn it seam side down, and cover the bowl with oiled plastic wrap. Mark the time with a felt-tipped pen on the plastic wrap and allow the dough to rest and rise in a moderately cool place until the dough has doubled in volume, 1 to 2 hours, depending on the heat of your environment.

After the first 30 minutes of fermentation, turn the dough out of the bowl onto your work surface, and fold a second time as described above. Return the dough to the bowl, cover, and complete the fermentation.

CUT, PRE-SHAPE, REST, AND SHAPE Once the dough has doubled in volume, sprinkle a little more flour onto your work surface, then scrape the dough out onto it and let the dough assume its natural shape. Dust the top of the dough with a little flour and pat it down gently, then use a metal bench scraper or a knife to divide it into two 15-ounce pieces.

Pre-shape the dough into logs as described on page 7, then cover them with oiled plastic wrap and let them rest for 10 minutes before you continue shaping.

Shape the dough into 2 filones, following the instructions on page 57.

PROOF Couche the filones on a floured towel on a baking sheet, following the instructions on page 39. Cover the filones with oiled plastic wrap and let them proof until the dough has doubled in volume, 30 to 40 minutes.

While the shaped dough is proofing, preheat the oven to 480°F, with an empty pan for creating steam on the bottom of the oven. Have ready a spritzer filled with water near the oven and approximately 8 ounces of hot water to pour into the empty pan.

After the dough has finished proofing, transfer the filones to an oiled baking sheet. Dust a bit of flour on the top to help keep the soft dough from tearing. Spritz the dough heavily with water and sprinkle the sesame seeds on top.

BAKE Open the oven door, and working quickly, slide the baking sheet with the filones onto the middle rack and pour the hot water into the empty pan below to create steam before quickly closing the oven door. After 1 minute, open the oven door, spritz around the dough, then close the door again.

The filones should bake to a golden brown in about 40 minutes.

COOL Let the filones cool on a wire rack. When the bread has cooled, use a serrated knife to cut the bread in two, and take a look inside.

Smell the sweet and nutty aromas from the durum wheat and toasted sesame seeds. The crumb will be delicate and lacy, with an open network of holes and a lovely soft yellow hue.

OTHER SHAPES TO TRY

You could shape this dough into four small, fat batards (see page 58), which make wonderful hoagie rolls for authentic Italian meatball sandwiches. Let the smaller batards proof for 25 to 35 minutes, and bake for 35 minutes.

BUILDING BREADS WITH A SOURDOUGH CULTURE

Creating an authentic sourdough culture to leaven your dough instead of using commercial yeast is the alchemy of bread making. If you begin at the beginning and get to know yeast in its wildest form, and then learn how to tame it, you'll have a deeper understanding of how the flavors of sourdough breads are dependent on the subtlest of changes during the fermentation of your culture. Creating the particular tang and tartness of sourdough, then rounding that sharpness into a full-flavored bread, is the ultimate goal, and respecting and managing the sourdough process from start to finish proves a baker's mettle.

We will start by creating a "white" sourdough culture. Each day, it is "fed" with organic white bread flour, except for the first day, when organic rye flour, which has more nutrients than white flour, helps to kick-start the fermentation process. This single culture will be the foundation for generating three breads: a sourdough white, a sourdough whole wheat, and a sourdough rye, each with a flavor profile unique to its particular grain.

These three breads are simple manifestations of this white sourdough culture, and the flavors and textures should be pleasing and addictive. From here, you may want to try making sourdough cultures using whole wheat and rye flours, and later in this book you will find additional and more challenging sourdough recipes.

After all, what is both complicated and satisfying about creating sourdough is the metamorphosis of the living yeast cultures into aromas and flavors that tug at the elemental in all of us, making bread into something that grounds us in a soulful way.

My simple goal here is to introduce the concept of making a sourdough bread from start to finish, and in the most basic of ways. But before we get to basic, there is just a little chemistry to understand.

MAKING A SOURDOUGH CULTURE TO LEAVEN YOUR DOUGH

Wild yeasts are the agents of creation for a sourdough culture. They are minute, one-celled spores belonging to the fungi group. Wild yeasts can be found in the surrounding environment of bread bakeries, in bags of organic flour (because of the lack of pesticides), in the soil, and on the skins of grapes and other fruits. Wild yeasts feed on flour and water and thrive in ambient temperatures of 74° to 76°F.

The first steps for building a successful sourdough culture are to capture and feed these wild yeasts. Once they are contained, the wild yeasts grow and multiply with scheduled feedings of flour and water. An ecosystem is formed with colonies of yeasts and bacteria, and in this environment the yeasts begin to live in symbiosis with a bacterium called lactobacillus. The lactobacillus feeds on the by-products from the yeast fermentation, and in turn, is responsible for producing the lactic acid that causes the sour taste of the culture.

Keeping in mind that to start the seed of life of authentic sourdough bread is a fragile undertaking no matter what, there are certain requirements necessary to ensure the health and growth of this culture. To avoid contaminants, the flour should be organic, and the water should be bottled and non-carbonated.

This formula for a sourdough culture can be made with organic white, whole wheat, or rye flour (beginning on the second day, using rye for the first day in all three versions). The recipe and process for developing these sourdough cultures are the same. You will need a clear 1-quart container with lid, a long-handled plastic or wooden spoon (not metal, which reacts with the acidity of the sourdough), a long-handled plastic spatula, and a diary and pen for scheduling feedings.

To produce a healthy culture that will leaven a dough takes time and patience because of the intricacies of creating a starter with a proper pH balance. The culture must become acidic enough to have a pronounced flavor in the bread, but it must remain balanced enough to not break down and destroy the gluten structure.

During the 10-day growth period, the looks and smells of fermentation change on a daily basis. After 10 days, the culture should be expansive, with a ripe smell, a healthy color, and an even network of bubbles. It can continue to be fed and used on a regular basis, or it can go dormant in your refrigerator and be refreshed with feedings before baking again.

DIARY OF A SOURDOUGH CULTURE

I began my adventure in all things sourdough by growing three sourdough cultures using white flour, whole wheat flour, and rye flour. The following excerpts from my "sourdough journal" are examples of the types of culture characteristics you might encounter over 10 days of feeding. So enthralled was I in growing these cultures that, as you will see, my observations, and also those of friends who were curious, became less and less scientific and more and more poetic.

Day 3

WHITE CULTURE: Bubbly, stretchy and bouncy; smelled like stinky raw cheese

WHOLE WHEAT CULTURE: Smelled like pumpkin and oats

RYE CULTURE: High-rise bubbles; smelled like rich stout beer

Day 5

WHITE: Strong, sharp smell of cheese and apples

WHOLE WHEAT: Toasty, vegetal

RYE: An autumn forest after it rains

Day 7

WHITE: Frothy, milder, settled, appealing

WHOLE WHEAT: Fruit-flavored—honey, apples; delicious

RYE: Happy, big symphony

Day 10

WHITE: Balanced, mature aromas and flavors—ready to go

WHOLE WHEAT: Sweet, intense, honey-apple perfume; tangy and bitter

RYE: Aromas of apple, beer, soil

Sourdough Culture

Use organic flour and bottled water to avoid contaminants; the water temperature should be 70° to 75°F. The container that holds the starter should be approximately 1 quart—big enough to accommodate approximately four times the volume of the original culture due to the expansion from fermentation—and clear plastic or glass so that you can see and understand the culture growth. Scrub it clean and rinse it well before use and make sure it has a lid.

YIELD
5 to 6 ounces for each sourdough bread made

Organic rye flour (to start)	4 ounces
Water (bottled, non-carbonated)	4 ounces, plus 4 ounces each day
Organic white bread flour, whole wheat flour, or rye flour	4 ounces each day

WEIGH Weigh the 4 ounces of organic rye flour into a medium bowl and make a well in the center.

Weigh 4 ounces of water into a second small bowl.

MIX Add the water to the flour, stir to incorporate completely, then scrape the mixture into the clear 1-quart container and cover loosely with the lid. Let ferment for 24 hours.

INSTRUCTIONS FOR DAILY FEEDING

Follow these instructions for 10 days, at which point the culture should be developed and strong enough to be able to leaven a dough. The second day of the culture's life is the first day of feeding, and the first day of 10 days.

To feed a culture means to add flour and water in a scheduled way. The feeding requirements for a healthy culture are a daily responsibility. In order to build a culture that is strong enough to leaven your dough, you must be disciplined in both the feeding times and in keeping your culture in a moderately warm environment, around 74°F. Make a note of the time of this first feeding and try to feed the culture at the same time every day. Keep a diary of daily changes and be aware of the extreme smells; these will peak and then subside. The goal is to find the balance where the assertive flavor meets the necessary strength to leaven your dough.

FIRST After 24 hours of allowing the flour and water mixture to ferment, stir the culture 8 to 10 times with a long-handled spoon. Before each daily feeding, it will be necessary to reduce the amount of culture in the container to 4 ounces: Use a spatula to scrape out the culture into a clean bowl. Place the empty container on your scale, tare it, then pour 4 ounces of the culture back into the container and discard the rest. The container does not need to be cleaned.

FEED Weigh 4 ounces of organic white bread flour (or whole wheat flour or rye flour) into the culture container. Weigh 4 ounces of water into the culture container.

MIX Stir the flour and the water into the culture to incorporate completely, then cover loosely with the lid. Let ferment for 24 hours.

Repeat, following these instructions, each day for 10 days.

By the tenth day, the culture should be nourished to the point of sustaining the life of a new dough. Look for a healthy froth of bubbling, bubbles that are consistently sized, and aromas that are tangy and fruity but not overtly acidic. Continue feeding the culture daily if you plan on actively using your sourdough culture to make bread. Or, you can put it to sleep and let the yeasts go dormant by placing the culture in your refrigerator, tightly covered, until you are ready to activate it again. It can keep for 3 to 4 weeks in the refrigerator, if not longer, but it will then need at least a week of resumed feedings before use.

To activate a dormant culture, remove the culture from the refrigerator, scrape off the liquid sludge accumulated at the top, and scrape out half of the starter, then put it on the feeding schedule as previously instructed. With a proper ambient temperature and daily feedings, the culture should come back to life within 1 to 2 weeks.

White Sourdough Boules

⫸ A note about using yeast for your first sourdough breads: I usually begin my first few doughs with a small amount of commercial yeast to provide a safety net, and start with the 5 ounces of sourdough culture in the formula given below. As you bake more loaves, you can wean yourself away from commercial yeast and balance the amount of sourdough starter with the salt in your recipe, adding more or less of each according to your own personal flavor preference. I find that 5 to 6 ounces of sourdough starter balances nicely with 2½ teaspoons of salt.

What's New

- A sourdough culture leavens the dough.
- The dough is shaped into boules.

THESE FIRST WHITE SOURDOUGH BOULES will be a smart starting point and a perfect canvas for the trial and error of understanding the balance and relationships of your ingredients. Take a photo of your sourdough culture and take notes about the flavor and acidity. Keep a watchful eye during all of the steps to get to know the behavior of this bread from start to finish; it may be slower to ferment and proof, but prolonged fermentation only enriches the flavors and textures.

Before you make your first sourdough bread: It is important to recognize that even with the recipe at hand, your first sourdough bread may slump in size, lack a zingy sour taste, or be pale and tight in color and texture. This is not unusual—this is how you learn, and making sourdough bread should always be considered a work in progress. The fun and satisfaction of making bread is really in the learning, doing, and tasting.

Active dry yeast (optional)	½ teaspoon
Table salt	2½ teaspoons
Warm water (if using active dry yeast)	1 ounce
Unbleached white bread flour	16 ounces
Sourdough culture (page 107; fed with white bread flour)	5 ounces
Cool water	10 or 11 ounces
Vegetable oil	

≫ If you choose to use the active dry yeast, you will need to dissolve it in the 1 ounce warm water. If you are not using the yeast, omit the warm water and instead increase the cool water to 11 ounces.

≫ The water temperature is especially important to help promote a healthy dough. The water temperature will probably fall within the range of 70° to 75°F, but as a reminder, here are the calculations to help you. To find the accurate water temperature, multiply as follows: 75 x 4 = 300. Now subtract the room temperature, flour temperature, sourdough temperature, and friction factor (see page 17) to get the appropriate water temperature for your dough.

≫ Due to the sticky nature of this dough, it may be a little tricky to fold, but continue as best you can, folding two or three times consecutively if possible, until the dough looks and feels supple and strong. You may need to let the dough relax for 5 minutes in between folds, and then flatten the dough and continue the process.

MEASURE AND WEIGH Measure the yeast, if using, and the salt separately and set them aside.

If using yeast, weigh the warm water into a small bowl. The warm water should feel hot to the touch, between 105° and 115°F. Sprinkle the yeast on top of the water, stir to dissolve, and set aside.

Weigh the flour into a large mixing bowl. Sprinkle the salt on top of the flour, stir to incorporate, and then make a well in the center.

Weigh the sourdough culture into a bowl and set aside.

Weigh the 10 ounces of cool water into a bowl, if using the yeast, or 11 ounces cool water if you are omitting the yeast.

MIX First, combine the sourdough culture with the cool water, using your fingers to help break up the culture so that it begins to dissolve in the water. If you are using the yeast, add the yeast mixture to the flour and stir 3 or 4 turns. Then, little by little, pour the cool water with the sourdough culture into the flour mixture. Mix with your hands for 2 to 3 minutes, until the water and the flour are incorporated, the grit of the salt is dissolved, and the dough forms a rough and shaggy mass, and then stop.

LET THE DOUGH REST Cover the bowl with a kitchen towel or plastic wrap and let the dough stand still for about 30 minutes.

FOLD Sprinkle your work surface with flour and then use a plastic bowl scraper to scrape the dough out onto it. Tap your hands in a little flour, then gently flatten the dough into a rectangle, with the short side facing you.

Use your fingers or the plastic scraper to flip the top edge of the dough down to just below the center, then flip the bottom edge up to just above the center. Repeat this process for the right and left sides, then turn the dough over and dust off the flour.

Fold the dough a second time, turn it over, and then fold a third time if possible.

FERMENT Oil a second large bowl, then place the dough in it, seam side up, to oil the top. Then turn it seam side down, and cover the bowl with oiled plastic wrap. Mark the time with a felt-tipped pen on the plastic wrap and allow the dough to rest and rise in a moderately cool place until it has doubled in volume, 1 to 2 hours, depending on the heat of your environment.

After the first 30 minutes of fermentation, turn the dough out of the bowl onto your work surface, and fold again as described on the previous page. Return the dough to the bowl, cover, and complete the fermentation.

CUT AND SHAPE Once the dough has doubled in volume, sprinkle a little more flour onto your work surface, then scrape the dough out onto it, letting the dough assume its natural shape. Divide the dough into 2 equal pieces and shape into boules following the instructions on pages 60 and 61.

PROOF Transfer the boules to an oiled baking sheet, cover with oiled plastic wrap, and let them proof until the dough has doubled in volume, 30 to 45 minutes.

While the shaped dough is proofing, preheat the oven to 480°F, with an empty pan for creating steam on the bottom of the oven. Have ready a spritzer filled with water near the oven and approximately 8 ounces of hot water to pour into the empty pan.

SCORE Once the boules have approximately doubled in volume, dust a little flour on top for a decorative look and smooth the flour gently with your hand. Dip a lame or straightedge razor in water, and score each boule with 4 cuts in a square, as pictured on page 114, cutting approximately ½ inch deep.

BAKE Open the oven door, and, working quickly, slide the baking sheet with the boules onto the middle rack and pour the hot water into the empty pan below to create steam before quickly closing the oven door. After 1 minute, open the oven door and spritz around the dough with water, then close the door again.

The boules should bake to a medium brown in 35 to 40 minutes.

Scoring a Simple Square

COOL Let the boules cool on a wire rack. After the bread has cooled, take a sharp knife and cut a slice off the end.

Check the interior development of the crumb, which should have evenly spaced small holes throughout, and smell and taste for a spike of sour aroma and flavor. The crumb should be moist, with a lovely sheen and an inviting, soft texture. The next sourdough breads in this chapter should also share these characteristics.

Words are not enough to explain the adventure of creating a living sourdough culture and developing a flavor component unique to your own environment. So no matter if your bread has or has not risen to its true potential: With all of the work you have completed leading to this chapter, you are now a true bread baker!

OTHER SHAPES TO TRY

You could also choose to make 3 or 4 baguettes, following the shaping instructions on pages 37 to 39. Proof, score, and bake as directed on pages 39 to 40.

Whole Wheat Sourdough Batards

WITH THE WHITE SOURDOUGH BOULES UNDER OUR BELTS, we can take the next step in our sourdough triumvirate and begin to enliven the flavor and texture by incorporating whole wheat flour into the dough and changing up the shape to batards. You could also use a whole wheat sourdough culture to lend more depth and character to this bread, as in the loaf on page 185.

YIELD
Approximately 32 ounces dough;
2 batards

Active dry yeast (optional)	½ teaspoon
Table salt	2½ teaspoons
Warm water (if using active dry yeast)	1 ounce
Unbleached bread flour	8 ounces
Whole wheat flour	8 ounces
Sourdough culture (page 107; fed with white bread flour or whole wheat flour)	5 ounces
Cool water	10 or 11 ounces
Vegetable oil	

≫ If you choose to use the active dry yeast, you will need to dissolve it in the 1 ounce warm water. If you are not using the yeast, omit the warm water and instead increase the cool water to 11 ounces.

MEASURE AND WEIGH Measure the yeast, if using, and the salt separately, and set them aside.

If using yeast, weigh the warm water into a small bowl. The warm water should feel hot to the touch, between 105° and 115°F. Sprinkle the yeast on top of the water, stir to dissolve, and set aside.

What's New

- Whole wheat flour is incorporated into the dough.
- The dough is shaped into batards.

Weigh the bread flour and whole wheat flour and combine in a large mixing bowl. Sprinkle the salt on top of the flour, stir to incorporate, and then make a well in the center.

Weigh the sourdough culture into a bowl and set aside.

Weigh the 10 ounces of cool water into a bowl, if using the yeast, or 11 ounces cool water if you are omitting the yeast.

MIX First, combine the sourdough culture with the cool water, using your fingers to help break up the culture so that it begins to dissolve in the water. If you are using the yeast, add the yeast mixture to the flour and stir 3 or 4 turns. Then, little by little, pour the cool water with the sourdough culture into the flour mixture. Mix with your hands for 2 to 3 minutes, until the water and the flour are incorporated, the grit of the salt is dissolved, and the dough forms a rough and shaggy mass, and then stop.

LET THE DOUGH REST Cover the bowl with a kitchen towel or plastic wrap and let the dough stand still for about 30 minutes.

FOLD Sprinkle your work surface with flour and then use a plastic bowl scraper to scrape the dough out onto it. Tap your hands in a little flour, then gently flatten the dough into a rectangle, with the short side facing you.

Use your fingers or the plastic bowl scraper to flip the top edge of the dough down to just below the center, then flip the bottom edge up to just above the center. Repeat this process for the right and left sides, then turn the dough over and dust off the flour.

Fold the dough a second time, turn it over, and then fold a third time if possible.

FERMENT Oil a second large bowl, then place the dough in it, seam side up, to oil the top. Then turn it seam side down, and cover the bowl with oiled plastic wrap. Mark the time with a felt-tipped pen on the plastic wrap and allow the dough to rest and rise in a moderately

The water temperature is especially important to help promote a healthy dough, and will probably fall within the range of 70° to 75°F, but as a reminder, here are the calculations to help you. To find the accurate water temperature, multiply as follows: 75 x 4 = 300. Now subtract the room temperature, flour temperature, sourdough temperature, and friction factor (see page 17) to get the appropriate water temperature for your dough.

Due to the sticky nature of this dough, it may be a little tricky to fold, but continue as best you can, folding two or three times consecutively if possible, until the dough looks and feels supple and strong. You may need to let the dough relax for 5 minutes in between folds, and then flatten the dough and continue the process.

cool place until it has doubled in volume, 1 to 2 hours, depending on the heat of your environment.

After the first 30 minutes of fermentation, turn the dough out of the bowl onto your work surface, and fold again as described above. Return the dough to the bowl, cover, and complete the fermentation.

CUT, PRE-SHAPE, REST, AND SHAPE Once the dough has doubled in volume, sprinkle a little more flour onto your work surface, then scrape the dough out onto it, letting the dough assume its natural shape. Divide the dough into 2 equal pieces. Pre-shape the dough into logs as described on page 7, then cover with oiled plastic wrap and let rest for 5 to 10 minutes before you continue shaping. Shape the logs into batards, following the instructions on page 58.

PROOF Transfer the batards to an oiled baking sheet, cover with oiled plastic wrap, and let proof until the dough has doubled in volume, 30 to 45 minutes.

While the shaped dough is proofing, preheat the oven to 480°F, with an empty pan for creating steam on the bottom of the oven. Have ready a spritzer filled with water near the oven and approximately 8 ounces of hot water to pour into the empty pan.

SCORE Once the batards have approximately doubled in volume, dust a little flour on top for a decorative look and smooth the flour gently with your hand. Dip a lame or straightedge razor in water, and score each batard with diagonal cuts, as pictured at left, leaving ¼ inch at either end cutting approximately ½ inch deep.

BAKE Open the oven door, and working quickly, slide the baking sheet with the batards onto the middle rack and pour the hot water into the empty pan below to create steam before quickly closing the oven door. After 1 minute, open the oven door and spritz around the dough with water, then close the door again.

The batards should bake to a medium brown in 35 to 40 minutes.

COOL Let the bread cool completely on a wire rack.

OTHER SHAPES TO TRY

You could also choose to make 2 filones, following the shaping instructions on page 57, and top them with a sprinkling of seeds such as sunflower or other healthy grains. Proof and bake as directed on pages 102 and 103.

Rye Sourdough Pan Loaf

ALTHOUGH THE SMALLER AMOUNT OF PROTEIN in rye flour can make it particularly challenging to construct a strong dough foundation, the earthy flavors and tastes drawn out from this grain make sourdough rye breads deeply pleasurable. Baking this first sourdough rye in a pan helps to keep the integrity of its shape.

YIELD
Approximately 32 ounces dough; one 9-by-5-inch loaf

Active dry yeast (optional)	½ teaspoon
Table salt	2½ teaspoons
Warm water (if using active dry yeast)	1 ounce
Unbleached bread flour	10 ounces
Rye flour	6 ounces
Sourdough culture (page 107; fed with white bread flour or rye flour)	5 ounces
Cool water	10 or 11 ounces
Vegetable oil	

If you choose to use the active dry yeast, you will need to dissolve it in the 1 ounce warm water. If you are not using the yeast, omit the warm water and instead increase the cool water to 11 ounces.

MEASURE AND WEIGH Measure the yeast, if using, and the salt separately and set them aside.

If using yeast, weigh the warm water into a small bowl. The warm water should feel hot to the touch, between 105° and 115°F. Sprinkle the yeast on top of the water, stir to dissolve, and set aside.

Weigh the bread flour and rye flour and combine them in a large mixing bowl. Sprinkle the salt on top of the flour, stir to incorporate, and then make a well in the center.

What's New
- Rye flour is incorporated into the dough.
- The dough is baked in a loaf pan.

The water temperature is especially important to help promote a healthy dough, and will probably fall within the range of 70° to 75°F, but as a reminder, here are the calculations to help you. To find the accurate water temperature, multiply as follows: 75 x 4 = 300. Now subtract the room temperature, flour temperature, sourdough temperature, and friction factor (see page 17) to get the appropriate water temperature for your dough.

Weigh the sourdough culture into a bowl and set aside.

Weigh the 10 ounces of cool water into a bowl, if using the yeast, or 11 ounces cool water if you are omitting the yeast.

MIX First, combine the sourdough culture with the cool water, using your fingers to help break up the culture so that it begins to dissolve in the water. If you are using the yeast, add the yeast mixture to the flour and stir 3 or 4 turns. Then, little by little, pour the cool water with the sourdough culture into the flour mixture. Mix with your hands for 2 to 3 minutes, until the water and the flour are incorporated, the grit of the salt is dissolved, and the dough forms a rough and shaggy mass, and then stop.

LET THE DOUGH REST Cover the bowl with a kitchen towel or plastic wrap and let the dough stand still for about 30 minutes.

FOLD Sprinkle your work surface with flour and then use a plastic bowl scraper to scrape the dough out onto it. Tap your hands in a little flour, then gently flatten the dough into a rectangle, with the short side facing you.

Use your fingers or the plastic bowl scraper to flip the top edge of the dough down to just below the center, then flip the bottom edge up to just above the center. Repeat this process for the right and left sides, then turn the dough over and dust off the flour.

Fold the dough a second time, turn it over, and then fold a third time if possible.

Due to the sticky nature of this dough, it may be a little tricky to fold, but continue as best you can, folding two or three times consecutively if possible, until the dough looks and feels supple and strong. You may need to let the dough relax for 5 minutes in between folds, and then flatten the dough and continue the process.

FERMENT Oil a second large bowl, then place the dough in it, seam side up, to oil the top. Then turn it seam side down, and cover the bowl with oiled plastic wrap. Mark the time with a felt-tipped pen on the plastic wrap and allow the dough to rest and rise in a moderately cool place until it has doubled in volume, 1 to 2 hours, depending on the heat of your environment.

After the first 30 minutes of fermentation, turn the dough out of the bowl onto your work surface, and fold again as described above. Return

the dough to the bowl, cover, and let rise for another 30 minutes, then fold again. After this last fold, return the dough to the bowl, cover, and complete the fermentation.

PRE-SHAPE, REST, AND SHAPE Once the dough has doubled in volume, sprinkle a little more flour onto your work surface, then scrape the dough out onto it, letting the dough assume its natural shape. Pre-shape the dough into a log as described on page 7, then cover with oiled plastic wrap and let rest for 5 to 10 minutes before you continue shaping. Shape into a batard, following the instructions on page 58. With the seam side down, place the batard into an oiled 9-by-5-inch loaf pan and gently press it into the corners.

PROOF Cover the pan with oiled plastic wrap and let the dough proof until doubled in size, 45 to 60 minutes.

While the dough is proofing, preheat the oven to 480°F, with a rack in the middle for baking and an empty pan for creating steam on the bottom of the oven. Have ready a spritzer filled with water near the oven and approximately 8 ounces of hot water to pour into the empty pan.

SCORE Once the pan loaf has approximately doubled in volume, dust a little rye flour on top for a decorative look and smooth the flour gently with your hand. Dip a lame or straightedge razor in water, and score the top with diagonal cuts, as pictured opposite, first in one direction, then in the opposite direction, leaving ¼ inch at either end and cutting approximately ½ inch deep.

BAKE Open the oven door, slide the loaf pan onto the middle rack, and pour the hot water into the empty pan below to create steam before quickly closing the oven door. After 1 minute, open the oven door and spritz around the dough, then close the door.

The loaf should bake to a dark brown in 40 to 50 minutes.

COOL When the bread has finished baking, let it stand for 10 minutes in the pan, then take it out of the pan and let it cool completely on a wire rack.

The weight and gravity of the dough in the pan mean this bread needs just a little push to reach the lovely arc of its potential. I bake this bread when it is a little shy of complete proof, just before it reaches a slightly curved top, because when the dough is underproofed, the oven spring will be greater.

OTHER SHAPES TO TRY

You could also choose to make small rolls of 2 to 3 ounces each, shaped as directed for boules on pages 60 to 61. Before baking, spritz them with water and top them with large crystal salt and caraway seeds. For proofing and baking times, follow the instructions for the ciabatta rolls on pages 84 to 85.

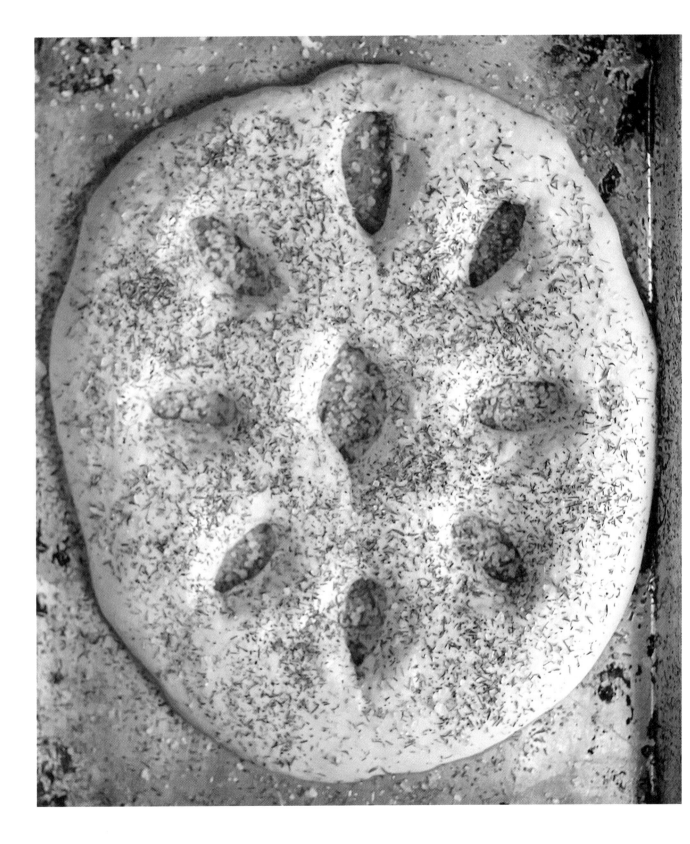

PART FOUR

BUILDING ON WHAT YOU'VE LEARNED

ASSEMBLING RECIPES WITH DISTINCTIVE INGREDIENTS AND SHAPES

I studied painting in college, and by my fourth year I was experimenting with abstract expressionism. But before I could break away into that ideational realm, I needed to have a grasp on the classic studies, such as how to draw the human figure and how to represent true perspective. This base of knowledge lent substance to my canvases—and it's really no different for any field of study. Now that you know the fundamentals of baking bread, you can explore new opportunities for artistry. This chapter eases you into recipes that push tastes and textures to develop in new ways.

Many of the following recipes begin with one of the ten classic doughs you have learned in the previous pages and evolve by ingredient or shape into something new. The baguette dough, for example, has enough strength to support many different shapes, and it can also be baked in a loaf pan. The pain de mie is something of a transition dough, similar to baguette dough but with the addition of milk and butter.

Focaccia can accommodate a variety of toppings, and it can also become the foundation for an entire meal, such as the classic pissaladière. Or it can be turned into a delicious breakfast or dessert bread by adding fruits and topping it with crunchy turbinado sugar. This dough's particular hydration encourages the stretch and pull of stellar new shapes, and it allows for decorative cuts such as those that define the magnificent fougasse. And it turns out that ciabatta dough can be extremely adaptable when it's handled properly, as you'll see in my crusty, densely crumbed Italian-style bread. Ciabatta also makes an excellent pizza crust and can, with very little effort, be turned into crackers that will begin any party with a bang.

The flavors of whole wheat, semolina, and rye flours are vibrant on their own and can be enhanced with preferments and soakers to incorporate the addition of ancient grains and toasted flours. Fruits and nuts add a punctuation to texture, but they are incorporated at the end of mixing. (These ingredients can pierce and tear the strands of gluten and destroy the structure that allows fermentation to occur, so they must be handled with a bit more care.)

The exceptional flavor sensations of sourdough attract uncommon ingredients to create well-balanced but supremely flavorful breads. The tang of whole wheat sourdough tastes of autumn and melds with dried fruits and rosemary, while rye sourdough has notes of summer and becomes inspired with the addition of briny Kalamata olives sprinkled with lemon zest. These creative combinations are both fun and delicious, and with the skills you have mastered from the previous chapters, it's easy to make all of these recipes. Use them as your departing point to spur you on to create *your* own signature breads.

Country White Loaf

AN OILED 9-BY-5-INCH PAN is the only additional requirement to turn baguette dough into a sandwich loaf. By baking this dough in a pan, you will see how manipulating the same dough in a different way affects the texture: This bread will have a more tender crumb than the baguette and will not be as crusty. Take your baguette dough through to full fermentation, then follow the shaping, proofing, and baking instructions below.

> **YIELD**
> 28 to 30 ounces dough;
> one 9-by-5-inch loaf

Unbleached bread flour, for dusting

Baguette dough (page 35 or page 67),
fully fermented

Vegetable oil

PRE-SHAPE, REST, AND SHAPE Once the dough has doubled in volume, sprinkle a little more flour onto your work surface, then scrape the dough out onto it, letting the dough assume its natural shape. Pre-shape the dough into a log as described on page 7, then cover with oiled plastic wrap and let rest for 5 to 10 minutes before you continue shaping. Shape into a batard, following the instructions on page 58. With the seam side down, place the batard into an oiled 9-by-5-inch loaf pan and gently press it into the corners.

PROOF Cover the loaf with oiled plastic wrap and let it proof until it has doubled in size, 50 to 60 minutes.

While the dough is proofing, preheat the oven to 450°F, with a rack in the middle for baking and an empty pan for creating steam on the bottom of the oven. Have ready a spritzer filled with water near the oven and approximately 8 ounces of hot water to pour into the empty pan.

>》》 The weight and gravity of the dough in the pan mean this bread needs just a little push to reach the lovely arc of its potential. I bake this bread when it is a little shy of complete proof, just before it reaches a slightly curved top, because when the dough is underproofed, the oven spring will be greater.

A high temperature at the beginning of baking helps this loaf rise to its maximum potential.

BAKE Once the pan loaf has approximately doubled in volume, dust a little flour on top for a decorative look and smooth the flour gently with your hand. This bread will be baked without scoring the top to promote an arced shape.

Open the oven door, slide the loaf pan onto the middle rack, and pour the hot water into the empty pan below to create steam before quickly closing the oven door. After 1 minute, open the oven door and spritz around the dough, then close the door.

Bake for approximately 10 minutes, then lower the oven temperature to 430°F and continue to bake until the crust has a deep brown glow, another 20 to 25 minutes.

COOL When the bread has finished baking, let it stand for 10 minutes in the pan, then take it out of the pan and let it cool completely on a wire rack.

Cinnamon-Raisin Pan Loaf

FOUNDATION DOUGH: Baguette

TAKE THE WHITE PAN LOAF on page 129 even further by adding a swirl of raisins and cinnamon and dusting it with crunchy turbinado sugar, for a delicious bread worth waking up to in the morning.

YIELD
Approximately 38 ounces dough;
One 9-by-5-inch loaf

Ground cinnamon	2 tablespoons
Granulated sugar	1 ounce
Raisins	8 ounces
Very hot water	8 ounces
Unbleached bread flour, for dusting	
Baguette dough (page 35 or page 67), fully fermented	
Vegetable oil	
Egg yolk, for egg wash	1
Water, for egg wash	1 ounce
Turbinado sugar	1 tablespoon (optional)

PREP THE RAISINS AND CINNAMON SUGAR Combine 1 tablespoon of the cinnamon and the granulated sugar in a small bowl, mix together, and set aside. Weigh the raisins into a small bowl and set aside.

Measure the hot water into a second small bowl that will be large enough to hold the raisins. Add the remaining 1 tablespoon cinnamon to the water and mix thoroughly, let sit for 1 minute, then add the raisins. The water should just cover the raisins; add more if necessary. Let the raisins steep for 1 minute, then drain them. It's important to dry

Hydrating the raisins lends more plumpness to the fruit and more moisture to the bread. Don't steep the raisins for too long, or the flavor will wash away, and make sure to use a paper towel to dry them, not a cloth towel, as the cinnamon will stain.

Ingredients like raisins or nuts can damage the gluten structure if they are added during the actual mixing, so here they are added during shaping instead.

the raisins a little, so pat them between pieces of paper towel, where they can remain until you are ready to add them to the dough.

SHAPE Sprinkle a little flour onto your work surface, then scrape the fully fermented dough out onto it, letting the dough assume its natural shape. Tap your hands in flour, and gently flatten the dough into a large, even rectangle of approximately 12 by 8 inches and 1 inch thick, with the short side facing you.

Spread a handful of the raisins evenly across the dough and gently press them into the dough. Repeat with the rest of the fruit.

Beginning with the end farthest from you, roll up the dough into a tight log. Tuck in the outer ends each time you roll. When you reach the end of the dough, seal the edge as you would a batard (see page 58), making sure the dough will easily fit into your pan. With the seam side down, place the dough into an oiled 9-by-5-inch loaf pan and gently press it into the corners.

PROOF Cover the loaf with oiled plastic wrap and let it proof until it has doubled in volume, 50 to 60 minutes.

While the dough is proofing, preheat the oven to 450°F, with a rack in the middle for baking and an empty pan for creating steam on the bottom of the oven. Have ready a water spritzer filled with water near the oven and approximately 8 ounces of hot water to pour into the empty pan.

Make an egg wash by stirring together the egg yolk and the water in a small bowl until well incorporated. Set aside until the loaf is ready to bake.

BAKE Brush the top of the loaf with the egg wash, then sprinkle the cinnamon sugar on top. For extra crunch and sweetness, if desired, sprinkle the turbinado sugar across the top. Open the oven door, slide the loaf pan onto the middle rack, and pour the hot water into the empty pan below to create steam before quickly closing the oven door. After 1 minute, open the oven door and spritz around the dough, then close the door.

Bake for approximately 10 minutes, then lower the oven temperature
to 430°F and continue to bake until the crust has a deep brown glow,
another 20 to 25 minutes.

COOL When the bread has finished baking, let it stand for 10 minutes
in the pan, then take it out of the pan and let it cool completely on a
wire rack.

Couronne of White Rolls

FOUNDATION DOUGH: Baguette

YIELD
28 to 30 ounces dough;
12 to 14 rolls

IN MAKING A *COURONNE*, or "crown," out of individual white rolls, the sum definitely becomes greater than the parts. Make this shape for an occasion or a holiday dinner—use it on the table as a centerpiece decoration before plucking the rolls away to eat.

Unbleached bread flour, for dusting

Baguette dough (page 35 or page 67),
fully fermented

Vegetable oil

≫ As you weigh each roll on the scale, you may need to add small pieces of dough to reach the 2-ounce weight. Add each small piece to the top of the roll, then gently tuck in the pieces and fold the dough over to incorporate them.

CUT, REST, AND SHAPE Sprinkle a little flour onto your work surface, and scrape the fully fermented dough out onto it, letting the dough assume its natural shape. Tap your hands in flour, gently flatten the dough, and then cut into twelve to fourteen 2-ounce pieces.

Let the cut rolls rest under oiled plastic wrap for 5 to 10 minutes. Shape these pieces into round rolls, following the instructions for shaping a boule on pages 60 and 61, and place them on a lightly oiled baking sheet in a circle; they should be tightly placed together and touching.

PROOF Cover the rolls with oiled plastic wrap and let proof until doubled in volume, 20 to 30 minutes.

While the shaped dough is proofing, preheat the oven to 450°F, with a rack in the middle for baking and an empty pan for creating steam on the bottom of the oven. Have ready a spritzer filled with water near the oven and approximately 8 ounces of hot water to pour into the empty pan.

SCORE Once the rolls have approximately doubled in volume, dust a little flour on top for a decorative look and smooth the flour gently with your hand. Dip a lame or straightedge razor in water, and score each roll with a simple line, as pictured on the previous page, approximately ½ inch deep.

BAKE Open the oven door, and, working quickly, slide the baking sheet with the rolls onto the middle rack and pour the hot water into the empty pan below to create steam before quickly closing the oven door. After 1 minute, open the oven door and spritz around the dough with water, then close the door again.

Bake for approximately 10 minutes, then lower the temperature to 430°F and continue to bake until the rolls are golden brown, about another 20 minutes.

COOL When the couronne has finished baking, let it stand for 10 minutes on the baking sheet, then carefully lift the couronne onto a wire rack to cool completely.

OTHER SHAPES TO TRY

You could make two smaller couronnes of 6 or 7 rolls each, or bake the rolls separately as dinner rolls. The proofing and baking times will be the same.

Pain de Mie

FOUNDATION DOUGH: Baguette

PAIN DE MIE MEANS "bread of the crumb" in French, and it's called that because of how the bread is baked; the vessel that holds the dough creates a finished product with very little crust and almost all crumb. The butter and milk make this a soft and malleable dough, which is supported by the pan it's baked in. The pan used for baking, called *pullman* because it replicates the shape of a railway car, is long and rectangular with a removable top, and is sold at specialty food stores (use a 15¾-by-3¾-inch size for this recipe). However, I've had luck by using a regular loaf pan and covering the top tightly with a lightly oiled piece of aluminum foil, doubled and wrapped snugly around the pan. This lovely bread with a tight and tender crumb is an excellent sandwich bread, and it also makes the perfect base for hors d'oeuvres when cut into small squares or triangles.

YIELD
Approximately 32 ounces dough;
One 15¾-by-3¾-inch or 9-by-5-inch loaf

Butter	2 ounces
Active dry yeast	1½ teaspoons
Sugar	1 tablespoon
Table salt	2 teaspoons
Warm water	1.75 ounces
Unbleached all-purpose flour	16 ounces
Milk	12 ounces
Vegetable oil	

MEASURE AND WEIGH Measure or weigh the butter, cut it into ½-inch cubes, and allow it to come to room temperature.

Measure the yeast, sugar, and salt separately and set them aside.

Weigh the warm water into a small bowl. The warm water should feel hot to the touch, between 105° and 115°F. Sprinkle the yeast on top of the water, stir to dissolve, and set aside.

Weigh the flour into a large mixing bowl. Sprinkle the salt and sugar on top of the flour, stir to incorporate, and then make a well in the center.

Weigh the milk into a small bowl.

MIX Add the yeast mixture and then the milk to the flour, mix the dough to incorporate, then add the butter. Continue mixing for 2 to 3 minutes in order to develop the gluten network.

> The mixture will a little feel dry before the butter is added; mix the butter between your fingers until it dissolves into the flour.

LET THE DOUGH REST Cover the bowl with a kitchen towel or plastic wrap and let the dough stand still for about 30 minutes.

FOLD Sprinkle your work surface with flour and then use a plastic bowl scraper to scrape the dough out onto it. Tap your hands in a little flour, then gently flatten the dough into a rectangle, with the short side facing you.

Use your fingers or the plastic scraper to flip the top edge of the dough down to just below the center, then flip the bottom edge up to just above the center. Repeat this process for the right and left sides, then turn the dough over and dust off the flour.

> Using all-purpose flour (instead of bread flour), milk, butter, and sugar noticeably changes the characteristics of this dough: The all-purpose flour has a lower protein content and lessens the strength of the gluten, while the protein in the milk helps to protect this more tender dough structure. Both the milk and butter add moisture and flavor, and the butter also helps to tenderize the crumb while promoting a longer shelf life. Sugar is a flavor component and enhances the caramelization of the crust.

FERMENT Oil a second large bowl, then place the dough in it, seam side up, to oil the top. Then turn it seam side down, and cover the bowl with oiled plastic wrap. Mark the time with a felt-tipped pen on the plastic wrap and allow the dough to rest and rise in a moderately cool place until it has doubled in volume, 1 to 2 hours, depending on the heat of your environment.

PRE-SHAPE, REST, AND SHAPE Once the dough has doubled in volume, sprinkle a little more flour onto your work surface, then scrape the dough out onto it, letting the dough assume its natural shape. Pre-shape the dough into a log as described on page 7, then cover with oiled plastic wrap and let rest for 5 to 10 minutes before you continue shaping. Shape into a batard, following the instructions on page 58. With the seam side down, place the dough into an oiled 15¾-by-3¾-inch pullman pan or 9-by-5-inch loaf pan and gently press it into the corners.

PROOF Cover the pan with oiled plastic wrap and let proof for 30 to 45 minutes, or until just before the dough reaches the top of the pan.

While the shaped dough is proofing, preheat the oven to 400°F, with a rack in the middle.

BAKE After the dough has finished proofing, remove the plastic wrap. If you are using a pullman pan, slide on the lid. If you are using a loaf pan, take a long piece of foil, oil the area that will come into contact with the dough, and wrap the foil tightly around the pan twice. Place the loaf pan on the middle rack of the oven and bake the bread for about 30 minutes.

Toward the end of the 30 minutes, pull the bread out of the oven and remove the lid or foil, then return the bread to the oven to continue baking until the top is a light brown color, 10 to 15 minutes.

COOL Remove the pan from the oven and let the bread rest in the pan for about 10 minutes, then unmold the bread and let it cool on a wire rack.

The oven temperature is significantly lower, as a slower and more moderate oven spring will allow the dough to better fill in the space of the sealed pan. We don't use an empty pan and water to create steam or spritz this dough.

Fougasse

FOUNDATION DOUGH: Focaccia

FOUGASSE IS A DERIVATION OF FOCACCIA, the only difference being in how the dough is shaped. For this bread, using a dough with a preferment really only changes the strength and extensibility of the dough; with either dough, the focus of the flavor will be the olive oil, salt, and thyme. Here is where a simple addition of decorative cuts makes a spectacular bread that will have everyone talking—about its beauty as well as its delicious taste.

YIELD
Approximately 30 ounces dough;
1 large oval fougasse

Unbleached bread flour, for dusting	
Focaccia dough (page 44 or page 74), fully fermented	
Olive oil	2 tablespoons
Dried thyme	2 tablespoons
Coarse salt	1 tablespoon

PRE-SHAPE, REST, AND SHAPE Once the dough has doubled in volume, sprinkle a little more flour onto your work surface, then scrape the dough out onto it, letting the dough assume its natural shape. Pre-shape the dough into a boule as described on pages 60 and 61, then transfer to a baking sheet, cover with oiled plastic wrap, and let rest for 20 to 30 minutes. Leaving the plastic on top of the dough, gently flatten it into a large oval, approximately 1 inch thick; see **(A)**, next page. Remove the plastic wrap. Use a sharp knife to cut nine 1- to 2-inch slits in the fougasse, one in the center and then 8 evenly spaced slits radiating from the center **(B)**. The cuts should be clean, not ragged, and should allow a border of 1 to 2 inches of dough at the edge. Cover the dough with oiled plastic wrap and let it relax for 15 minutes, then pull the cuts open so that each one forms a clean oval shape (C).

PROOF Cover the dough with plastic wrap and let it proof for 15 to 20 minutes. While the dough is proofing, preheat the oven to 450°F, with a rack in the middle for baking and an empty pan for creating steam on the bottom of the oven. Have ready a spritzer filled with water near the oven and approximately 8 ounces of hot water to pour into the empty pan.

Shaping a Fougasse

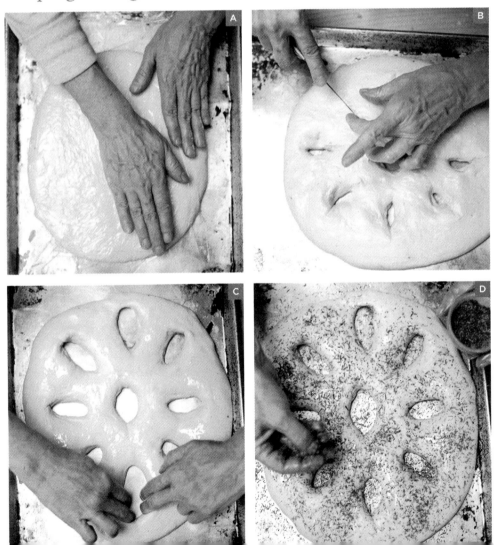

After the dough has finished proofing, lightly pat the olive oil onto the dough with a pastry brush (brushing on the oil can tear the dough) and sprinkle the thyme and the salt on top **(D)**. Gently press the ingredients into the dough.

BAKE Open the oven door, and, working quickly, slide the baking sheet with the fougasse onto the middle rack and pour the hot water into the empty pan below to create steam before quickly closing the oven door. After 1 minute, open the oven door and spritz around the dough with water, then close the door again.

Bake for approximately 30 minutes, until the fougasse is evenly browned.

COOL When the bread has finished baking, let it stand for 10 minutes, then remove it from the baking sheet and let it cool completely on a wire rack.

Classic Pissaladière

FOUNDATION DOUGH: Focaccia

PISSALADIÈRE IS A WONDERFUL FRENCH TREAT, described as a Provençal pizza, with the delicious combination of olives or olive paste, caramelized onions, anchovies, and a hint of thyme. The name comes from *pissala*, a fish paste made from anchovies. This recipe uses focaccia dough for the crust. Because the onions take some time to caramelize, prep them and your other ingredients while the dough is fermenting.

YIELD
Approximately 30 ounces dough;
One 17-by-12-inch rectangle

Medium yellow onions	6
Olive oil	2 to 4 tablespoons, plus more for the baking sheet
Anchovy fillets	24
Focaccia dough (page 44), fully fermented	
Olive paste	6 ounces
Dried thyme	2 tablespoons

PREP THE TOPPING Slice the onions into ¼-inch-thick slices. Heat a heavy skillet, cast iron if possible, over high heat and add 1 to 2 tablespoons oil (enough to coat the skillet), then add the onions. Cook, stirring every 2 to 3 minutes, for 5 to 6 minutes. Turn the heat to low and continue to cook the onions until they are medium brown and very soft, approximately 25 minutes. Transfer the onions to a paper towel–lined plate to cool. Rinse and pat dry the anchovies. Reserve 12 whole fillets, and coarsely chop the remaining 12.

SHAPE Once the dough has doubled in volume, oil an 18-by-13-inch rimmed baking sheet with olive oil and scrape the dough onto it, letting the dough relax into its own shape.

Drizzle 1 to 2 tablespoons of oil over the top of the dough, then use your fingertips to gently press and dimple the dough, distributing the oil and stretching and pushing the dough into the corners of the baking sheet.

PROOF Because your dough is topped with olive oil, it does not need to be covered. Let it proof on the baking sheet until doubled in volume, 30 to 45 minutes.

While the dough is proofing, preheat the oven to 450°F, with a rack in the middle for baking and an empty pan for creating steam on the bottom of the oven. Have ready a spritzer filled with water near the oven and approximately 8 ounces of hot water to pour into the empty pan.

BAKE Once the shaped dough has approximately doubled in volume, spread the olive paste and caramelized onions evenly across the dough and press them gently in, then add the chopped anchovies. Arrange the 12 whole anchovies in a decorative pattern around the edge and press them gently into the dough, then sprinkle the thyme across the top.

Open the oven door, and, working quickly, slide the baking sheet with the pissaladière onto the middle rack and pour the hot water into the empty pan below to create steam before quickly closing the oven door. After 1 minute, open the oven door and spritz around the dough with water, then close the door again.

The pissaladière should bake to a golden brown around the edges in 35 to 40 minutes.

COOL Let the pissaladière cool for 10 minutes on the baking sheet, then remove it from the pan and let it cool completely on a wire rack.

Focaccia with Red Onion, Asiago, and Thyme

FOUNDATION DOUGH: Focaccia

THIS IS A FOCACCIA that comes together with little muss or fuss, using simple ingredients that are easily found and assembled. With a salad it makes a delicious and simple Friday night dinner.

YIELD
Approximately 30 ounces dough;
one 17-by-12-inch rectangle

Medium red onions	2
Olive oil	2 to 3 tablespoons, plus more for the baking sheet
Bunch of fresh thyme	
Asiago cheese	2 ounces
Focaccia dough (page 44), fully fermented	

PREP THE TOPPING Slice the onions very thinly, then place in a bowl and toss with 1 tablespoon of the olive oil. Pull the thyme leaves from the stems. Grate the cheese.

SHAPE Once the dough has doubled in volume, oil an 18-by-13-inch rimmed baking sheet with olive oil and scrape the dough onto it, letting the dough relax into its own shape.

Drizzle 1 to 2 tablespoons olive oil over the top of the dough, then use your fingertips to gently press and dimple the dough, distributing the oil and stretching and pushing the dough evenly into the corners of the baking sheet.

PROOF Because your dough is topped with olive oil, it does not need to be covered. Let it proof on the baking sheet until doubled in volume, 30 to 45 minutes.

While the dough is proofing, preheat the oven to 450°F, with a rack in the middle for baking and an empty pan for creating steam on the bottom of the oven. Have ready a spritzer filled with water near the oven and approximately 8 ounces of hot water to pour into the empty pan.

BAKE Once the shaped dough has approximately doubled in volume, again use your fingertips to make dimples all over. Spread the onion mixture across the top, then sprinkle on the cheese, followed by the thyme, and press the ingredients gently into the dough.

Open the oven door, and, working quickly, slide the baking sheet with the focaccia onto the middle rack and pour the hot water into the empty pan below to create steam before quickly closing the oven door. After 1 minute, open the oven door and spritz around the dough with water, then close the door again.

The focaccia should bake to a golden brown in 35 to 40 minutes.

COOL Let the focaccia cool for 10 minutes on the baking sheet, then remove it from the pan and let it cool completely on a wire rack.

VARIATION: Focaccia with Lemon Slices, Tarragon, and Sea Salt This is one of my favorite toppings, especially in the spring and summer, both for the taste and for the lovely pattern of texture and color. Cut 4 lemons into very thin slices, as thin as you can possibly cut while still keeping each slice intact (a mandoline slicer is the best tool for this). Carefully remove the seeds. When the focaccia has finished proofing and is ready to bake, arrange the lemon slices on the top of the focaccia and press them into the dough. Sprinkle 2 teaspoons dried tarragon and 2 teaspoons coarse salt across the top, then bake as above.

Sweet Focaccia with Golden Raisins and Sour Cherries

FOUNDATION DOUGH: Focaccia

THIS SWEET FOCACCIA is loaded with tart cherries and golden raisins and topped with crunchy turbinado sugar. It's a recipe I developed when I worked at a bakery called Ecce Panis in New York City, and its sweet and tangy nature is delightful for breakfast, or with tea or coffee in the afternoon; my family especially enjoys it on Christmas morning. The sweet focaccia should have lovely purple-red tones from the cherries and a golden brown crust from the caramelization of the sugar.

YIELD
Approximately 48 ounces dough; one 17-by-12-inch rectangle or 14-inch round

Unsalted butter	2 ounces
Dried tart cherries	8 ounces
Golden raisins	8 ounces
Very hot water, for soaking the fruit	12 ounces
Active dry yeast	1½ teaspoons
Granulated sugar	2 teaspoons
Table salt	2 teaspoons
Warm water	1.75 ounces
Unbleached all-purpose flour	16 ounces
Walnut oil (or almond oil)	1 tablespoon, plus more for oiling the pan
Egg yolk, for egg wash	1
Water, for egg wash	2 ounces
Turbinado sugar, for sprinkling on top	2 ounces

I choose to use all-purpose flour to give the crumb of this bread a more tender quality, but bread flour also works.

MEASURE AND WEIGH Measure or weigh the butter and put it into the freezer for 15 to 20 minutes.

Weigh the cherries and the raisins into a bowl, mix together, then cover with the very hot water to hydrate for 30 to 60 seconds. Drain the fruit, reserving the soaking liquid for the dough. Add enough cool water to make 12 ounces, if necessary, and then refrigerate for 15 to 20 minutes, just until the liquid cools down to 70° to 75°F.

It's important to dry the raisins and cherries a little, so pat them between pieces of paper towel, where they can remain until you are ready to mix them into the dough.

Measure the yeast, granulated sugar, and salt separately and set them aside.

Weigh the warm water into a small bowl. The warm water should feel hot to the touch, between 105° and 115°F. Sprinkle the yeast on top of the water, stir to dissolve, and set aside.

Weigh the flour into a large mixing bowl. Sprinkle the sugar and the salt on top of the flour, then stir to incorporate.

MIX Take the butter from the freezer, and, holding it by the wrapper (or parchment paper or plastic wrap) on one end, grate it over the flour mixture using the medium holes of a grater until all the butter is in the bowl. (You made need to cut the last remaining piece with a knife to avoid grating your fingers.) With your fingers, working quickly, rub and blend the butter into the flour, then make a well in the center.

Add the yeast mixture to the flour, stir 3 or 4 turns, and then, little by little, add the reserved soaking liquid. Mix with your hands for 2 to 3 minutes, until all of the ingredients are incorporated, the grit of the salt and sugar is dissolved, and the dough forms a rough and shaggy mass, and then stop.

LET THE DOUGH REST Cover the bowl with a kitchen towel or plastic wrap and let the dough stand still for about 30 minutes.

≫ Using some of the fruity water in the dough adds a bit of sugar and sweetness, which will also push fermentation to be a little faster. It also contributes to the more intense color of the bread.

FOLD Sprinkle your work surface with flour and then use a plastic bowl scraper to scrape the dough out onto it. Tap your hands in a little flour, then gently flatten the dough into a rectangle, with the short side facing you.

Use your fingers or the plastic scraper to flip the top edge of the dough down to just below the center, then flip the bottom edge up to just above the center. Repeat this process for the right and left sides, then turn the dough over and dust off the flour.

FERMENT Oil a second large bowl with walnut oil (or almond oil), then place the dough in it, seam side up, to oil the top. Then turn it seam side down, and cover the bowl with oiled plastic wrap. Mark the time with a felt-tipped pen on the plastic wrap and allow the dough to rest and rise in a moderately cool place until it has doubled in volume, 1 to 2 hours, depending on the heat of your environment.

PRE-SHAPE, REST, AND SHAPE Once the dough has doubled in volume, sprinkle a little more flour onto your work surface, then scrape the dough out onto it and let the dough assume its natural shape. Dust the top of the dough with a little flour and pat it down gently into a large, even rectangle of approximately 12 by 8 inches and 1 inch thick, with the short side facing you.

Take a handful of cherries and raisins and spread them across the dough, gently pressing them down. Repeat with the remaining cherries and raisins until all of the fruit is pressed into the dough.

Use your fingers or the plastic scraper to flip the top edge of the dough down to just below the center, then flip the bottom edge up to just above the center. Repeat this process for the right and left sides, then turn the dough over and dust off the flour.

Let the dough relax for 5 minutes, then fold again as above.

Cover the dough with oiled plastic wrap and let rest for 20 to 30 minutes. Then oil an 18-by-13-inch rimmed baking sheet or other pan with walnut oil or almond oil and transfer the dough to the pan.

⫸ Folding the dough twice helps to evenly distribute the fruit.

An 18-by-13-inch rimmed baking sheet will accommodate this dough nicely, as will a large round pan. I use an oven-safe flat paella pan, 14 inches in diameter, which suits this dough perfectly. Depending on the type and size of pan, your finished bread will vary a little in thickness.

OTHER SHAPES TO TRY

You could also choose to bake the focaccia in two 10- to 12-inch round cake pans. The proofing and baking times will be the same.

Drizzle 1 tablespoon of walnut oil over the top of the dough, then use your fingertips to gently press and dimple the dough, distributing the oil and stretching and pushing the dough evenly into the pan.

PROOF Because your dough is topped with walnut oil, it does not need to be covered. Let it proof until doubled in volume, 30 to 45 minutes.

While the dough is proofing, preheat the oven to 400°F, with a rack in the middle for baking and an empty pan for creating steam on the bottom of the oven. Have ready a spritzer filled with water near the oven and approximately 8 ounces of hot water to pour into the empty pan.

Make an egg wash by stirring together the egg yolk and water until well incorporated. Set aside until ready to bake.

BAKE Once the shaped dough has approximately doubled in volume, again use your fingertips to make only the slightest dimples all over the dough. Use a pastry brush to pat the top with the egg wash and sprinkle the turbinado sugar evenly across.

Open the oven door, and, working quickly, slide the baking sheet or pan onto the middle rack and pour the hot water into the empty pan below to create steam before quickly closing the oven door. After 1 minute, open the oven door and spritz around the dough with water, then close the door again.

The sweet focaccia should bake to a golden brown in 30 to 35 minutes.

COOL Let the bread cool for 10 minutes on the baking sheet or pan, then remove and let cool completely on a wire rack.

Sarah's Signature Italian Bread

FOUNDATION DOUGH: Ciabatta

THE EXTRA WATER IN CIABATTA DOUGH lends itself to making thin, crisp pizzas as well as lovely light crackers, but before we get to these fun breads, I hope you'll attempt to make my signature Italian bread, so beautiful that it almost looks like a burnished metal sculpture. But what makes this bread worthwhile is that the formidable shape and thick crust disguise a uniquely delicate, moist yet toothsome interior crumb. For best results, I like to bake this dough on a baking stone (see page 15 for more information on using a baking stone).

YIELD
Approximately 32 ounces dough;
1 large oval loaf

Unbleached bread flour, for dusting

Ciabatta dough (page 50 or page 80),
fully fermented

Vegetable oil

Cornmeal, for the baking stone

SHAPE Sprinkle a little flour onto your work surface, then scrape the fully fermented dough out onto it, letting it assume its natural shape. Dust the top of the dough with a little flour and pat it down gently.

Shape the ciabatta into 1 large boule following the instructions on pages 60 and 61.

PROOF Cover the boule with oiled plastic wrap and let it proof until doubled in volume, 30 to 35 minutes.

⧉ This dough, although sloppy, is easy enough to shape into a boule, but because of its slack nature, it will then relax into a looser version of a boule, which is what you want.

While the dough is proofing, preheat the oven to 480°F, with a baking stone on the middle rack and an empty pan for creating steam on the bottom of the oven. Have ready a spritzer filled with water near the oven, approximately 8 ounces of hot water to pour into the empty pan, and about ½ cup of cornmeal, or a mixture of half cornmeal and half flour, for the baking stone.

≫≫ Both stretching the ciabatta and turning the dough upside down elongate and open up air pockets in the dough.

Sprinkle the back of an inverted baking sheet heavily with flour. Once the dough has approximately doubled in volume, very, very gently stretch the ciabatta boule to lengthen it to a graceful oval shape about 12 inches in length. As you finish, place the boule, upside down, on the floured back of the baking sheet.

BAKE Open the oven door, pull the rack with the baking stone toward you, and sprinkle the stone with the cornmeal. Working quickly and guiding the dough with one hand, shuttle the ciabatta boule from the back of the baking sheet onto the stone, then pour the hot water into the empty pan below to create steam before quickly closing the oven door. After 1 minute, open the oven door and spritz *around* the ciabatta *but not on top of the dough,* to keep the decorative flour markings intact.

The ciabatta should bake to a very dark brown in 45 to 50 minutes.

COOL Let the ciabatta cool completely on a wire rack.

Pizza

FOUNDATION DOUGH: Ciabatta

CIABATTA DOUGH CAN BE THE BASIS for a traditional pizza, though the shaping may require less aggressive stretching and pulling techniques than you might see at your local pizzeria. The "pie" is the limit in terms of what ingredients you want to use to top your pizza, but here is a version with simple yet delicious toppings. A baking stone (see page 15) promotes a thin, crispy pizza crust.

YIELD
Approximately 32 ounces dough; two 8-inch pizzas

Unbleached bread flour, for dusting	
Ciabatta dough (page 50 or page 80), fully fermented	
Vegetable oil	
Cornmeal, for the baking stone	
Cherry tomatoes	20
Bunch of fresh rosemary	
Olive oil	2 tablespoons
Black or green olive paste	4 ounces
Parmesan cheese, grated	4 ounces

SHAPE (1) Once the dough has doubled in volume, sprinkle a little more flour onto your work surface, then scrape the dough out onto it, letting the dough assume its natural shape. Divide the dough into 2 equal pieces and shape into boules following the instructions on pages 60 and 61.

》》 Both ciabatta dough and focaccia dough are extensible enough to use as a pizza base; ciabatta, as a more highly hydrated dough, can be stretched to become a thinner crust.

≫ You will not need an empty pan on the bottom of the oven for steam. We will not steam or spritz the pizzas in order to keep the crust from rising too high.

PROOF Cover the boules with oiled plastic wrap and let them relax and proof until doubled in size, approximately 30 minutes.

While the dough is proofing, preheat the oven to 480°F, with a baking stone on the middle rack. Have about ½ cup of cornmeal, or a mixture of half cornmeal and half flour, at the ready so it can be easily and quickly sprinkled on the stone.

During this time, prep your toppings: Cut the cherry tomatoes in half and pull some rosemary leaves off the stems; reserve 2 sprigs.

SHAPE (2) After the boules have proofed, flour your hands and the work surface, and pat the first boule into a flat circle, then press the heel of your hand all around the dough to make a rise at the crust's edge. Lift the dough so it drapes over the knuckles of both hands, and then gently rotate the dough to expand the diameter until it's approximately 8 inches. If you are feeling confident, twist and toss once or twice in the air, as this efficiently and gently stretches the gluten into a larger circle.

Repeat with the second boule, placing the stretched dough on the back of a baking sheet sprinkled with flour. If your stone is large enough to accommodate both pizzas, you can bake them both at once. If not, refrigerate the second piece of dough (without the toppings), covered with oiled plastic wrap, until the first pizza is finished baking.

BAKE Tap the olive oil onto the dough using a pastry brush, spread the olive paste across the dough, and place the cherry tomatoes on the dough. Sprinkle with the Parmesan cheese and some rosemary leaves. Open the oven door, pull the rack with the baking stone toward you, and sprinkle the stone with the cornmeal. Shuttle the pizza(s) from the baking sheet onto the stone and quickly close the oven door.

Bake until the crust is light brown in color, approximately 25 minutes. Top with a sprig of rosemary in the center. If you baked only one pizza, enjoy it immediately while you make the second pizza.

Crackers

FOUNDATION DOUGH: Ciabatta

MANIPULATING CIABATTA DOUGH by pulling it into a thin, pliable layer that stretches across the baking sheet makes a cracker-like foundation, ready for any kind of topping. I like to infuse olive oil with different herbs, but plain olive oil works just as well to flavor the crackers and keep them crisp. Specialty ingredients such as smoked salt and unique spices can be found more and more easily; I shop at Spices and Tease in Chelsea Market in NYC, but search online for your favorite toppings to find retail locations near you or to purchase them online. For variations on this recipe, try sprinkling the dough with caraway or sesame seeds, Parmesan or Asiago cheese, or even turbinado sugar for a sweet rendition.

YIELD
Approximately 32 ounces dough;
2 to 4 large crackers (filling
2 baking sheets)

Unbleached bread flour, for dusting	
Ciabatta dough (page 50 or page 80), fully fermented	
Vegetable oil	
Olive oil	2 tablespoons
Mild soft goat cheese, at room temperature	2 to 3 ounces
Caraway seeds	2 tablespoons

CUT AND PRE-SHAPE Sprinkle flour onto your work surface, and scrape the fully fermented dough out onto it, letting it assume its natural shape. Tap your hands in flour, and gently flatten the dough into a large, even rectangle approximately 12 by 8 inches and 1 inch thick,

then use a metal bench scraper or a knife to divide it into 2 or 4 equal pieces. Shape each piece into a log as described on page 7.

PROOF Cover the logs with oiled plastic wrap, and let them proof until doubled in size, approximately 30 minutes.

While the dough is proofing, preheat the oven to 450°F, with one rack at the top and one in the middle for baking.

SHAPE Pull and stretch each log into a flat rectangle, as thin as possible without tearing it, and place it on an oiled baking sheet. You should be able to fill 2 baking sheets, with 1 large or 2 smaller crackers per sheet. While stretching the dough, allow it to rest for 5 minutes in between stretches so that the gluten relaxes and the dough does not contract and tear.

Using a pastry brush, pat each cracker with 1 tablespoon olive oil. Use a spoon to gently smooth dabs of goat cheese evenly across each cracker, then sprinkle with the caraway seeds.

BAKE Slide the baking sheets into the oven and quickly close the oven door.

Bake for 10 to 14 minutes, until the crackers begin to brown evenly. Rotate the baking sheets in the oven halfway through baking if the crackers begin to brown too quickly in one spot. The crackers should be ¼ to ½ inch thick, and crispy, and are best eaten immediately (you won't be able to resist them for long, anyway!). To serve, break the crackers into different-size pieces and pile into a basket or on top of a platter along with a small bowl of olive oil for dipping.

VARIATIONS: Follow the instructions above, but top with olive oil and 1) a mix of dried herbs with large-crystal sea salt, or 2) smoked salt. For a sweet rendition, press the seeds from 1 pomegranate into the dough and sprinkle with pomegranate sugar (available at Spices and Tease) and/or turbinado sugar. These sweetish crackers go well with a glass of Champagne at New Year's.

≫ As when making pizza (page 162), you will not need a spritzer or an empty pan in the bottom of the oven for creating steam; this dough will not be spritzed or steamed.

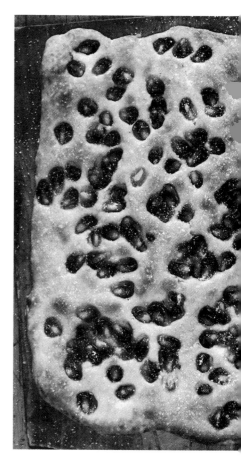

Whole Wheat Sandwich Bread with Lavender Honey

FOUNDATION DOUGH: Whole Wheat Pain de Campagne

YIELD
Approximately 30 ounces dough;
one 9-by-5-inch loaf

FOLLOWING ON YOUR EXPERIENCE of working with whole wheat flour to make Pain de Campagne (page 87), we will simplify the process, making a light and tasty whole wheat sandwich bread without a preferment, but with the addition of lavender-infused honey, the lavender and the honey pairing perfectly with the whole wheat and adding a bit of sweetness and moisture to the crumb. The lavender adds a unique taste, but if it's not for you, simply leave it out. If you want to omit the honey entirely, add an ounce or two more water.

Honey	1 ounce
Culinary lavender buds	¼ teaspoon
Active dry yeast	1½ teaspoons
Table salt	2 teaspoons
Warm water	1.75 ounces
Unbleached bread flour	6 ounces
Whole wheat flour	10 ounces
Cool water	10 ounces
Canola oil	1 ounce

MEASURE AND WEIGH Weigh the honey into a small saucepan, then measure the lavender and add it to the honey. Heat over low heat, stirring, until the honey becomes a little more liquid, 2 to 3 minutes. Remove from the heat and let the lavender steep in the honey as it cools. (Leave the lavender in the honey.)

Measure the yeast and salt separately and set them aside.

Weigh the warm water into a small bowl. The warm water should feel hot to the touch, between 105° and 115°F. Sprinkle the yeast on top of the water, stir to dissolve, and set aside.

Weigh the bread flour and the whole wheat flour and combine them in a large mixing bowl. Sprinkle the salt on top of the flour, stir to incorporate, and then make a well in the center.

Weigh the cool water into a small bowl. The cool water temperature should be between 70° and 75°F.

Weigh the canola oil into a small bowl.

MIX Add the yeast mixture to the flour, stir 3 or 4 turns, and then, little by little, add the cool water, followed by the honey with the lavender and the canola oil. Mix with your hands for 2 to 3 minutes, until all of the ingredients are incorporated, the grit of the salt is dissolved, and the dough forms a rough and shaggy mass, and then stop.

LET THE DOUGH REST Cover the bowl with a kitchen towel or plastic wrap and let the dough stand still for about 30 minutes.

FOLD Sprinkle your work surface with flour and then use a plastic bowl scraper to scrape the dough out onto it. Tap your hands in a little flour, then gently flatten the dough into a rectangle, with the short side facing you.

Use your fingers or the plastic bench scraper to flip the top edge of the dough down to just below the center, then flip the bottom edge up to just above the center. Repeat this process for the right and left sides, then turn the dough over and dust off the flour.

FERMENT Oil a second large bowl, then place the dough in it, seam side up, to oil the top. Then turn it seam side down, and cover the bowl with oiled plastic wrap. Mark the time with a felt-tipped pen on the plastic wrap and allow the dough to rest and rise in a moderately cool place until it has doubled in volume, 1 to 2 hours, depending on the heat of your environment.

SHAPE Once the dough has doubled in volume, sprinkle a little more flour onto your work surface, then scrape the dough out onto it, letting the dough assume its natural shape. Pre-shape the dough into a log as described on page 7, then cover with oiled plastic wrap and let rest for 5 to 10 minutes before you continue shaping. Shape into a batard, following the instructions on page 58. With the seam side down, place the dough into an oiled 9-by-5-inch loaf pan and gently press it into the corners.

PROOF Cover the dough with oiled plastic wrap and let it proof for 50 to 60 minutes, or until the dough has doubled in volume.

While the dough is proofing, preheat the oven to 450°F, with a rack in the middle for baking and an empty pan for creating steam on the bottom of the oven. Have ready a spritzer filled with water near the oven and approximately 8 ounces of hot water to pour into the empty pan.

SCORE Once the pan loaf has approximately doubled in volume, dust a little flour on top for a decorative look and smooth the flour gently with your hand. Dip a lame or straightedge razor in water, and score with 1 long cut down the center, leaving ½ inch on either end and cutting ½ inch deep.

BAKE Open the oven door, slide the loaf pan onto the middle rack, and pour the hot water into the empty pan below to create steam before quickly closing the oven door. After 1 minute, open the oven door and spritz around the dough, then close the door.

Bake for approximately 10 minutes, then lower the temperature to 430°F and continue to bake until the crust has a deep brown glow, another 20 to 25 minutes.

COOL When the bread has finished baking, let it stand for 10 minutes in the pan, then take it out of the pan and let it cool completely on a wire rack.

The weight and gravity of the dough in the pan mean this bread needs just a little push to reach the lovely arc of its potential. I bake this bread when it is a little shy of complete proof, just before it reaches a slightly curved top, because when the dough is underproofed, the oven spring will be greater.

OTHER SHAPES TO TRY

This particular recipe can also be made into 3 or 4 small baguettes, each 12 to 14 inches long: Follow the baguette instructions for shaping through to baking on pages 37 to 40. Make a little extra lavender honey to spread across a buttered warm baguette.

Whole Wheat Rolls with Toasted Grains and Currants

FOUNDATION DOUGH: Whole Wheat Pain de Campagne

YIELD
Approximately 48 ounces dough;
approximately 24 rolls

THIS DELICIOUS WHEAT BREAD benefits from toasting a portion of the whole wheat flour in the oven, which highlights the rich flavor of the grain. The toasted flour is used as half of the total flour for the preferment, and as a small percentage of the flour for the dough. Currants complement the earthy flavors of the grain and add just the right bit of sweetness, but you can also top this bread with a pinch of turbinado sugar to round out the flavor. I like to shape these into two different shapes, oval and round rolls, and pile them into a bread basket for the dinner table or as a gift for a bread-loving friend.

PÂTE FERMENTÉE (MAKES 8 OUNCES)

Whole wheat flour	3 ounces
Active dry yeast	¾ teaspoon
Table salt	1½ teaspoons
Warm water	1 ounce
Unbleached bread flour	2 ounces
Cool water	2 ounces

Whole Wheat Rolls

Whole wheat flour	8 ounces
Currants	8 ounces
Very hot water	8 ounces
Cool water	8 ounces
Active dry yeast	1 teaspoon
Table salt	2 teaspoons
Warm water	1.75 ounces
Unbleached bread flour	8 ounces
Honey	1 ounce
Pâte Fermentée (opposite)	8 ounces
Turbinado sugar (optional)	2 tablespoons

TOAST THE FLOUR Preheat the oven to 350°F. Weigh the 3 ounces of whole wheat flour for the pâte fermentée and 2 ounces of the whole wheat flour for the dough (5 ounces total), and spread the flour evenly on a baking sheet. Toast for 8 to 10 minutes, until the flour turns light brown. Set the flour aside to cool before using it.

> ≫ Toasting the flour changes its bonding ability and strength. When you mix the dough, some of the strands will not form; instead, the dough will clump and break a little. For this reason, we only toast a small percentage of the flour.

Pâte Fermentée

MEASURE AND WEIGH Measure the yeast and the salt separately and set them aside.

Weigh the warm water into a small bowl. The warm water should feel hot to the touch, between 105° and 115°F. Sprinkle the yeast on top of the water, stir to dissolve, and set aside.

Weigh the bread flour into a medium mixing bowl. Measure 3 ounces of the toasted whole wheat flour and add it to the bowl. Sprinkle the salt on top of the flour, stir to incorporate, and then make a well in the center.

Weigh the cool water into a small bowl.

MIX Add the yeast mixture to the flour, then the cool water, and stir until all of the ingredients are incorporated, the grit of the salt is dissolved, and the pâte fermentée forms a rough and shaggy mass, and then stop.

FERMENT Cover the bowl with oiled plastic wrap and mark the time with a felt-tipped pen on the plastic wrap. Allow the pâte fermentée to rest and rise in a moderately cool place until it has doubled in volume, 1 to 2 hours, depending on the heat of your environment.

Whole Wheat Rolls

PREP THE CURRANTS Weigh the currants into a small bowl that will also be large enough to hold the hot water to cover them, and set aside.

Measure the hot water and pour over the currants. The water should just cover the currants; add more if necessary. Let them steep for 30 to 60 seconds, then drain them, reserving the currant soaking liquid. It's important to dry the currants a little, so pat them between pieces of paper towel, where they can remain until you are ready to add them to the dough.

Add 4 ounces of the reserved soaking liquid to the cool water to make a total of 12 ounces liquid; discard the rest of the soaking liquid.

MEASURE AND WEIGH Measure the yeast and the salt separately and set them aside.

Weigh the warm water into a small bowl. The warm water should feel hot to the touch, between 105° and 115°F. Sprinkle the yeast on top of the water, stir to dissolve, and set aside.

Weigh the bread flour and whole wheat flour, including the reserved 2 ounces toasted whole wheat flour, and combine them in a large mixing bowl. Sprinkle the salt on top of the flours, stir to incorporate, and then make a well in the center.

Weigh the honey into a small bowl.

⫸ Depending on your schedule, the pâte fermentée can be placed in the refrigerator after 45 minutes to complete fermentation. It can be held for 12 hours before you need to proceed with making the bread.

⫸ Hydrating the currants lends more plumpness to the fruit and more moisture to the bread. Don't steep the currants for too long, or the flavor will wash away, and make sure to use a paper towel to dry them, not a cloth towel. Using some of the fruity water in the dough adds a bit of sugar and sweetness, which will also push fermentation to be a little faster.

MIX First, combine the pâte fermentée with the fruity cool water, using your fingers to help break it up to dissolve. Add the yeast mixture to the flour, stir 3 or 4 turns, and then, little by little, add the cool water with the pâte fermentée, followed by the honey. Mix with your hands for 2 to 3 minutes, until all of the ingredients are incorporated, the grit of the salt is dissolved, and the dough forms a rough and shaggy mass, and then stop.

LET THE DOUGH REST Cover the bowl with a kitchen towel or plastic wrap and let the dough stand still for about 30 minutes.

FOLD Sprinkle your work surface with flour and then use a plastic bowl scraper to scrape the dough out onto it. Tap your hands in a little flour, then gently flatten the dough into a rectangle, with the short side facing you.

Use your fingers or the plastic scraper to flip the top edge of the dough down to just below the center, then flip the bottom edge up to just above the center. Repeat this process for the right and left sides, then turn the dough over and dust off the flour.

FERMENT Oil a second large bowl, then place the dough in it, seam side up, to oil the top. Then turn it seam side down, and cover the bowl with oiled plastic wrap. Mark the time with a felt-tipped pen on the plastic wrap and allow the dough to rest and rise in a moderately cool place until it has doubled in volume, 1 to 2 hours, depending on the heat of your environment.

CUT AND SHAPE Once the dough has doubled in volume, sprinkle a little more flour onto your work surface, then scrape the dough out onto it and let the dough assume its natural shape. Dust the top of the dough with a little flour and pat it down gently into a large, even rectangle of approximately 12 by 8 inches and 1 inch thick, with the short side facing you.

Spread a handful of currants evenly across the dough and gently press them into the dough, then repeat with the rest of the currants.

This is a stiff dough, and with the addition of whole wheat flour it's going to take some patience and some muscle to incorporate all of the ingredients together. Take your time, stir with your hand from the center to pull the flours to you as the water is added, and bit by bit, the dough will form a mass. If the dough feels too dry, add another ounce or two of water.

Beginning with the end farthest from you, roll up the dough into a tight log. Tuck in the outer ends each time you roll. When you reach the end of the dough, seal the edge as you would a batard (see page 58), then let the dough rest for 10 minutes under oiled plastic wrap.

Use a metal bench scraper or a knife to cut the dough log into approximately twenty-four 2-ounce pieces. To shape these pieces into round and long rolls, follow the instructions for a boule on pages 60 and 61 and a batard on page 58, making a mix of both shapes as desired. Place the rolls on a lightly oiled baking sheet.

PROOF Cover with oiled plastic wrap and let the rolls proof until they have doubled in size, 25 to 30 minutes.

While the dough is proofing, preheat the oven to 450°F, with a rack in the middle for baking and an empty pan for creating steam on the bottom of the oven. Have ready a spritzer filled with water near the oven and approximately 8 ounces of hot water to pour into the empty pan.

SCORE Once the rolls have approximately doubled in volume, dip a lame or straightedge razor in water, and score the round rolls with a simple X and the long rolls with a cut down the middle, leaving approximately ⅛ inch on either end. If desired, spritz a little water on top and then sprinkle a fair amount of turbinado sugar on top of each roll.

BAKE Open the oven door, slide the baking sheet onto the middle rack, and pour the hot water into the empty pan below to create steam before quickly closing the oven door. After 1 minute, open the oven door and spritz around the rolls, then close the door.

Bake for approximately 10 minutes, then lower the temperature to 430°F and continue to bake until the rolls are golden brown, another 25 to 30 minutes.

COOL When the rolls have finished baking, remove them from the baking sheet and let them cool completely on a wire rack.

Rich Pumpernickel with Toasted Grains

FOUNDATION DOUGH: German Rye

AN ADDITION OF TOASTED PUMPERNICKEL flour is enhanced by both molasses and cocoa, taking the foundation of the German rye on page 93 three steps further. The very slight chocolate overtones and the sweetness from the molasses partner well with these grains, though the dough will be sticky to work with.

YIELD
Approximately 32 ounces dough;
4 mini batards

Pumpernickel flour	6 ounces
Active dry yeast	1½ teaspoons
Table salt	2 teaspoons
Unsweetened cocoa powder	¼ ounce
Warm water	1.75 ounces
Unbleached bread flour	8 ounces
Whole wheat flour	4 ounces
Cool water	9 ounces
Molasses	2 ounces
Vegetable oil	

TOAST THE PUMPERNICKEL FLOUR Preheat the oven to 350°F. Weigh the pumpernickel flour, spread it evenly on a baking sheet, and toast it in the oven until brown, 8 to 10 minutes. Let it cool completely before using. Weigh 4 ounces of this toasted flour and set aside for the dough. Reserve the remaining toasted flour for dusting the loaves before baking.

MEASURE AND WEIGH Measure and weigh the yeast, salt, and cocoa powder separately and set them aside.

Weigh the warm water into a small bowl. The warm water should feel hot to the touch, between 105° and 115°F. Sprinkle the yeast on top of the water, stir to dissolve, and set aside.

Weigh the bread flour and whole wheat flour, and combine in a large mixing bowl with the 4 ounces toasted pumpernickel flour. Sprinkle the cocoa powder and salt on top of the flour, stir to incorporate, and then make a well in the center.

Weigh the cool water into a small bowl, then the molasses into another small bowl. The cool water temperature should be between 70° and 75°F.

MIX Add the yeast mixture to the flour mixture, stir 3 or 4 turns, and then, little by little, add the cool water. Mix with your hands for 2 to 3 minutes, then add the molasses. Continue mixing until all of the ingredients are incorporated, the grit of the salt is dissolved, and the dough forms a rough and shaggy mass, and then stop.

LET THE DOUGH REST Cover the bowl with a kitchen towel or plastic wrap and let the dough stand still for about 30 minutes.

FOLD Sprinkle your work surface with flour and then use a plastic bowl scraper to scrape the dough out onto it. Tap your hands in a little flour, then gently flatten the dough into a rectangle, with the short side facing you.

Use your fingers or the plastic scraper to flip the top edge of the dough down to just below the center, then flip the bottom edge up to just above the center. Repeat this process for the right and left sides, then turn the dough over and dust off the flour.

FERMENT Oil a second large bowl, then place the dough in it, seam side up, to oil the top. Then turn it seam side down, and cover the bowl with oiled plastic wrap. Mark the time with a felt-tipped pen on the plastic wrap and allow the dough to rest and rise in a moderately cool place until it has doubled in volume, 1 to 2 hours, depending on the heat of your environment.

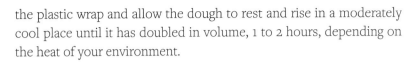

Because pumpernickel flour is low in protein, this dough benefits from additional folding, which develops strength.

After the first 30 minutes of fermentation, turn the dough out of the bowl onto your work surface, and fold again as described on the previous page. Return the dough to the bowl, cover, and complete the fermentation.

CUT, PRE-SHAPE, REST, AND SHAPE Once the dough has doubled in volume, sprinkle a little more flour onto your work surface, then scrape the dough out onto it, letting the dough assume its natural shape. Dust the top of the dough with a little flour and pat it down gently. Divide the dough into 4 equal pieces, then pre-shape them into logs as described on page 7. Let the dough rest for about 10 minutes, then shape the logs into batards, following the instructions on page 58.

PROOF To proof the mini batards, take a kitchen towel about the size of your baking sheet, and place it on top of the baking sheet. Tuck the left edge of the towel under itself, then sprinkle the entire towel heavily with flour. Place the first batard, seam side down, on top of the towel at the very left end and the second batard below it. Pull the towel on the right toward the batard to form a loop up against the dough. Place the third and fourth batards on the towel next to the first two, and pull the towel to make another loop. Finish by tucking the right-hand edge of the towel under itself. Cover with oiled plastic wrap and let the batards proof until the dough has doubled in volume, 30 to 40 minutes.

While the shaped dough is proofing, preheat the oven to 480°F, with an empty pan for creating steam on the bottom of the oven. Have ready a spritzer filled with water near the oven and approximately 8 ounces of hot water to pour into the empty pan in the oven to create steam.

SCORE Once the batards have approximately doubled in volume, transfer them to a baking sheet. Dust a little of the reserved toasted pumpernickel flour on top for a decorative look and smooth the flour gently with your hand. Dip a lame or straightedge razor in water, and score with curved lines as pictured opposite.

BAKE Open the oven door, slide the baking sheet with the batards onto the middle rack, and pour the hot water into the empty pan below to create steam before quickly closing the oven door. After 1 minute, open the oven door and spritz around the batards, then close the door.

The mini batards should bake in 30 to 35 minutes.

COOL Let the batards cool completely on a wire rack.

OTHER SHAPES TO TRY

You could also make two medium batards of 16 ounces each, extending the proof and baking times by 5 to 10 minutes each (couche the larger batards as you would the minis). Because this dough is more fragile, it's difficult to make any shape larger than these.

Semolina Ciabatta

FOUNDATION DOUGH: Italian Semolina

YIELD
Approximately 32 ounces dough;
4 small rectangular loaves, each
approximately 8 by 4 inches

THIS SEMOLINA CIABATTA is similar to the semolina bread on page 99, but it uses no butter and requires more water, plus an awareness of how to work with this highly hydrated dough. Your first lesson in ciabatta on page 50 will serve you well here to achieve lightness of crumb from this heavier grain.

Active dry yeast	1½ teaspoons
Table salt	2 teaspoons
Warm water	1.75 ounces
Unbleached bread flour	8 ounces
Durum flour	8 ounces
Cool water	14 ounces
Vegetable Oil	

MEASURE AND WEIGH Measure the yeast and the salt separately and set them aside.

Weigh the warm water into a small bowl. The warm water should feel hot to the touch, between 105° and 115°F. Sprinkle the yeast on top of the water, stir to dissolve, and set aside.

Weigh the bread flour and durum flour and combine them in a large mixing bowl. Sprinkle the salt on top of the flour, stir to incorporate, and then make a well in the center.

Weigh the cool water into a small bowl. The cool water temperature should be between 70° and 75°F.

MIX Add the yeast mixture to the flour, stir 3 or 4 turns, and then, little by little, add the cool water. Mix with your hands for 2 to 3 minutes, until all of the ingredients are incorporated, the grit of the salt is dissolved, and the dough forms a mass, and then stop.

LET THE DOUGH REST Cover the bowl with a kitchen towel or plastic wrap and let the dough stand still for about 30 minutes.

FOLD Sprinkle your work surface with flour and then use a plastic bowl scraper to scrape the dough out onto it. Tap your hands in a little flour, then gently flatten the dough into a rectangle, with the short side facing you.

Use your fingers or the plastic scraper to flip the top edge of the dough down to just below the center, then flip the bottom edge up to just above the center. Repeat this process for the right and left sides, then turn the dough over and dust off the flour.

This wet dough will benefit from a second fold; let the dough relax for 1 to 2 minutes after the first fold, then sprinkle a little more flour on your work surface and fold a second time.

FERMENT Oil a second large bowl, then place the dough in it, seam side up, to oil the top. Then turn it seam side down, and cover the bowl with oiled plastic wrap. Mark the time with a felt-tipped pen on the plastic wrap and allow the dough to rest and rise in a moderately cool place until the dough has doubled in volume, 1 to 2 hours, depending on the heat of your environment.

After the first 30 minutes of fermentation, turn the dough out of the bowl onto your work surface, and fold again as described above. Return the dough to the bowl, cover, and complete the fermentation.

CUT AND SHAPE Once the dough has doubled in volume, sprinkle a lot of flour onto your work surface, and prepare a proofing place for the ciabatta by sprinkling the same amount of flour on the back of an inverted baking sheet.

Check the water absorption of the flour mixture; if the dough is too dry, add another ounce or two of water.

Use the plastic scraper to scrape the dough out onto the work surface, letting it assume its natural shape. Tap your hands in flour, and gently flatten the dough into a large, even rectangle of approximately 12 by 8 inches and 1 inch thick.

Use a metal bench scraper or knife to cut the dough into four equal pieces, approximately 6 inches long and 4 inches wide. Gently place them on the floured back of the baking sheet.

PROOF Cover the ciabatta with oiled plastic wrap and let proof until the dough has doubled in volume, 30 to 45 minutes.

While the shaped dough is proofing, preheat the oven to 480°F, with an empty pan for creating steam on the bottom of the oven. Have ready a spritzer filled with water near the oven and approximately 8 ounces of hot water to pour into the empty pan.

Once the dough has approximately doubled in volume, sprinkle more flour on the work surface. Work with 1 ciabatta piece at a time and stretch it very gently to lengthen it to approximately 8 inches, then place it on the floured area of your counter. Dust off your baking sheet and oil it, and place each ciabatta piece upside down on the baking sheet.

BAKE Open the oven door, and, working quickly, slide the baking sheet with the ciabatta onto the middle rack, then pour the hot water into the empty pan below to create steam before quickly closing the oven door. After 1 minute, open the oven door and spritz around the dough with water, then close the door again.

The semolina ciabatta should bake to a very dark brown in 40 to 45 minutes.

COOL Let the semolina ciabatta cool completely on a wire rack.

As the pieces of ciabatta proof on the floured surface, they will pick up a pattern of flour that will show with beautiful striations once the loaves are turned over to bake.

Semolina Bread with Toasted Pecans

FOUNDATION DOUGH: Italian Semolina

DURUM FLOUR, BUTTER, AND PECANS all lend sweetness to this bread. Besides being amazingly delicious, the golden color of the durum wheat matched with the dark bits of toasted pecans makes it beautiful to look at, too.

YIELD
Approximately 38 ounces dough;
2 batards

Pecan halves	9 ounces
Unbleached bread flour, for dusting	
Italian Semolina dough (page 99), fully fermented	
Vegetable oil	

TOAST THE PECANS Preheat the oven to 375°F. Weigh the pecans onto a baking sheet, spread the nuts evenly across it, and bake for 8 to 12 minutes, until the nuts are dark brown. Set aside to cool completely, then coarsely chop.

PRE-SHAPE, REST, CUT, AND SHAPE Sprinkle a little flour onto your work surface, then scrape the fully fermented dough out onto it, letting the dough assume its natural shape. Tap your hands in flour, and gently flatten the dough into a large, even rectangle of approximately 12 by 8 inches and 1 inch thick, with the short side facing you.

Spread a handful of the pecans evenly across the dough and gently press them in, then repeat with the rest of the pecans.

To fold the dough, use your fingers or a plastic bowl scraper to flip the top edge of the dough down to just below the center, then flip the bottom edge up to just above the center. Repeat this process for the right and left sides, then turn the dough over and dust off the flour.

Let the dough relax for 5 minutes, then fold again as above.

Cover the dough with oiled plastic wrap and let rest for 10 minutes, then use a metal bench scraper or a knife to divide it into 2 equal pieces. Shape the pieces into tight logs and seal the edges as you would for a batard, following the instructions on page 58.

PROOF Transfer to an oiled baking sheet, cover with oiled plastic wrap, and let the dough proof until doubled in size, approximately 30 minutes.

While the dough is proofing, preheat the oven to 480°F, with an empty pan for creating steam on the bottom of the oven. Have ready a spritzer filled with water near the oven and approximately 8 ounces of hot water to pour into the empty pan.

BAKE Open the oven door, and, working quickly, slide the baking sheet with the semolina batards onto the middle rack, then pour the hot water into the empty pan below to create steam before quickly closing the oven door. After 1 minute, open the oven door and spritz around the dough with water, then close the door again.

The semolina pecan bread should bake to a golden brown in 45 to 50 minutes.

COOL Let the bread cool completely on a wire rack.

Folding the dough twice helps to evenly distribute the pecans.

Whole Wheat Sourdough with Figs, Apples, and Raisins

FOUNDATION DOUGH: Whole Wheat Sourdough

THE UNIQUE FLAVOR OF SOURDOUGH here matches with uncommon ingredients to create a well-balanced but supremely flavored loaf of bread. To add to the thrust of flavor, rosemary-infused oil is brushed on top of the loaf, which is then sprinkled with turbinado sugar to balance the tang of the sour with sweet.

YIELD
Approximately 38 ounces dough; one 9-by-5-inch loaf

Olive oil	2 ounces
Dried rosemary	1 tablespoon
Dried figs	3 ounces
Dried apples	3 ounces
Raisins	3 ounces
Active dry yeast (optional)	½ teaspoon
Table salt	2 teaspoons
Warm water (if using active dry yeast)	1 ounce
Honey	1 ounce
Unbleached white bread flour	6 ounces
Whole wheat flour	6 ounces
Sourdough culture (page 107, fed with whole wheat flour)	5 ounces
Cool water	7 or 8 ounces
Vegetable Oil	
Turbinado sugar	1 ounce

≫ If you choose to use the active dry yeast, you will need to dissolve it in the 1 ounce warm water. If you are not using the yeast, omit the warm water and instead increase the cool water to 8 ounces.

PREP THE ROSEMARY OIL Weigh the olive oil into a small saucepan, then add the rosemary. Heat over low heat for 2 to 3 minutes, making sure the oil does not boil. Remove from the heat and let the rosemary steep in the cooling oil for at least 1 hour.

PREP THE FIGS, APPLES, AND RAISINS Weigh the figs, apples, and raisins. Coarsely chop the figs and the apples, and then combine the figs, apples, and raisins in a small bowl and mix together. Pour enough very hot water over the dried fruit to just cover. Let the fruit steep for 30 seconds, then drain, discarding the liquid. It's important to dry the fruit a little, so pat it between pieces of paper towel, where it can remain until you are ready to add it to the dough.

MEASURE AND WEIGH Measure the yeast, if using, and the salt separately and set them aside.

Weigh the warm water, if using, into a small bowl. The warm water should feel hot to the touch, between 105° and 115°F. Sprinkle the yeast on top of the water, stir to dissolve, and set aside.

Weigh the honey into a small bowl and set aside.

Weigh the bread flour and whole wheat flour and combine in a large mixing bowl. Sprinkle the salt on top of the flour, stir to incorporate, and then make a well in the center.

Weigh the sourdough culture into a bowl and set aside. Weigh the 7 ounces of cool water into a bowl, if using the yeast, or 8 ounces cool water if you are omitting the yeast.

MIX First, combine the sourdough culture with the cool water, using your fingers to help break it up to dissolve. If you are using the yeast, add the yeast mixture to the flour and stir 3 or 4 turns. Then, little by little, add the cool water with the culture, followed by the honey. Mix with your hands for 2 to 3 minutes, until all of the ingredients are incorporated, the grit of the salt is dissolved, and the dough forms a rough and shaggy mass, and then stop.

The water temperature is especially important to help promote a healthy dough, and it will probably fall within the range of 70° to 75°F, but as a reminder, here are the calculations to help you. To find the accurate water temperature, multiply as follows: 75 x 4 = 300. Now subtract the room temperature, flour temperature, sourdough culture temperature, and friction factor (see page 17) to get the appropriate water temperature for your dough.

LET THE DOUGH REST Cover the bowl with a kitchen towel or plastic wrap and let the dough stand still for about 30 minutes.

FOLD Sprinkle your work surface with flour and then use a plastic bowl scraper to scrape the dough out onto it. Tap your hands in a little flour, then gently flatten the dough into a rectangle, with the short side facing you.

Use your fingers or the plastic scraper to flip the top edge of the dough down to just below the center, then flip the bottom edge up to just above the center. Repeat this process for the right and left sides, then turn the dough over and dust off the flour.

Fold the dough a second time, turn it over, and then fold a third time if possible.

FERMENT Oil a second large bowl, then place the dough in it, seam side up, to oil the top. Then turn it seam side down, and cover the bowl with oiled plastic wrap. Mark the time with a felt-tipped pen on the plastic wrap and allow the dough to rest and rise in a moderately cool place until it has doubled in volume, 1 to 2 hours, depending on the heat of your environment.

After the first 30 minutes of fermentation, turn the dough out of the bowl onto your work surface, and fold again as described above. Return the dough to the bowl, cover, and complete the fermentation.

SHAPE Once the dough has doubled in volume, sprinkle a little more flour onto your work surface, then scrape the dough out onto it, letting the dough assume its natural shape. Tap your hands in flour, and gently flatten the dough into a large, even rectangle of approximately 12 by 8 inches and 1 inch thick with the short side facing you.

Spread a handful of the fruit evenly across the dough and gently press the fruit into the dough. Repeat with the rest of the fruit.

Beginning with the end farthest from you, roll up the dough into a tight log. Tuck in the outer ends each time you roll. When you reach the end

Due to the sticky nature of this dough, it may be a little tricky to fold, but continue as best you can, folding two or three times consecutively if possible, until the dough looks and feels supple and strong. You may need to let the dough relax for 5 minutes in between folds, then flatten the dough and continue the process.

of the dough, seal the edge as you would a batard (see page 58). With the seam side down, place the dough into an oiled 9-by-5-inch loaf pan and gently press it into the corners, then brush the top of the loaf with some of the rosemary oil.

PROOF Cover the loaf with plastic wrap and let proof until the dough has doubled in volume, 45 to 60 minutes.

While the shaped dough is proofing, preheat the oven to 450°F, with a rack in the middle of the oven and an empty pan for creating steam on the bottom of the oven. Have ready a spritzer filled with water near the oven and approximately 8 ounces of hot water to pour into the empty pan.

SCORE Once the loaf has approximately doubled in volume, brush the top with more rosemary oil. Any extra oil can be kept in a sealed container in your refrigerator for up to 1 week. Dip a lame or straightedge razor in water and score the loaf as pictured at left, with a single long straight line down the center and 6 to 8 short cuts on each side of the middle cut, angled away from the center, approximately ½ inch deep and leaving approximately ⅛ inch on either end. Sprinkle the top of the loaf heavily with the turbinado sugar.

BAKE Open the oven door, and, working quickly, slide the loaf pan onto the middle rack, then pour the hot water into the empty pan below to create steam before quickly closing the oven door. After 1 minute, open the oven door and spritz around the dough with water, then close the door again.

Bake for approximately 10 minutes, then lower the temperature to 430°F and continue to bake until the crust has a deep brown glow, another 30 to 35 minutes.

COOL When the bread has finished baking, let it stand for 10 minutes in the pan, then take it out of the pan and let it cool completely on a wire rack.

≫ The weight and gravity of the dough in the pan mean this bread needs just a little push to reach the lovely arc of its potential. I bake this bread when it is a little shy of complete proof, just before it reaches a slightly curved top, because when the dough is underproofed, the oven spring will be greater.

Sour Rye Rolls with Olives, Lemon Zest, and Celery Seed Salt

FOUNDATION DOUGH: Rye Sourdough

THIS BREAD IS A TRIPLE-SOUR DELIGHT, made with a rye sourdough culture, Kalamata olives, and lemon zest. The flavor is complex and intense, veering off in sharp tones from the sourdough, lemon, and olives, but balanced by the saltiness of the crust. The recipe is similar to the rye sourdough recipe on page 119, but here the amount of bread flour is increased to lend more stability.

YIELD
Approximately 36 ounces dough;
17 or 18 rolls

Lemon zest	from 1 lemon
Kalamata olives	9 ounces
Active dry yeast (optional)	½ teaspoon
Table salt	2½ teaspoons
Warm water (if using active dry yeast)	1 ounce
Unbleached bread flour	9 ounces
Rye flour	5 ounces
Sourdough culture (page 107, fed with rye flour)	5 ounces
Cool water	7 or 8 ounces
Vegetable oil	
Coarse salt, for topping the rolls	1 tablespoon
Celery seeds, for topping the rolls	1 tablespoon
Olive oil, for topping the rolls	2 tablespoons

⋙ If you choose to use the active dry yeast, you will need to dissolve it in the 1 ounce warm water. If you are not using the yeast, omit the warm water and instead increase the cool water to 8 ounces.

MEASURE AND WEIGH Zest the lemon and set aside. Weigh the olives, pit them, and chop into ½-inch pieces. Toss the olives with the lemon zest in a small bowl.

Measure the yeast and the table salt separately and set them aside.

Weigh the warm water, if using, into a small bowl. The warm water should feel hot to the touch, between 105° and 115°F. Sprinkle the yeast on top of the water, stir to dissolve, and set aside.

Weigh the bread flour and rye flour and combine in a large mixing bowl. Sprinkle the salt on top of the flour, stir to incorporate, and then make a well in the center.

Weigh the sourdough culture and set aside. Weigh the 7 ounces of cool water into a small bowl, if using the yeast, or 8 ounces cool water if you are omitting the yeast.

MIX First, combine the sourdough culture with the cool water, using your fingers to help break it up to dissolve. If you are using the yeast, add the yeast mixture to the flour and stir 3 or 4 turns. Then, little by little, add the cool water with the culture. Mix with your hands for 2 to 3 minutes, until all of the ingredients are incorporated, the grit of the salt is dissolved, and the dough forms a rough and shaggy mass, and then stop.

LET THE DOUGH REST Cover the bowl with a kitchen towel or plastic wrap and let the dough stand still for about 30 minutes.

FOLD Sprinkle your work surface with flour and then use a plastic bowl scraper to scrape the dough out onto it. Tap your hands in a little flour, then gently flatten the dough into a rectangle, with the short side facing you.

Use your fingers or the plastic bowl scraper to flip the top edge of the dough down to just below the center, then flip the bottom edge up to just above the center. Repeat this process for the right and left sides, then turn the dough over and dust off the flour.

The water temperature is especially important to help promote a healthy dough, and it will probably fall within the range of 70° to 75°F, but as a reminder, here are the calculations to help you. To find the accurate water temperature, multiply as follows: 75 x 4 = 300. Now subtract the room temperature, flour temperature, sourdough temperature, and friction factor (see page 17) to get the appropriate water temperature for your dough.

Due to the sticky nature of this dough, it may be a little tricky to fold, but continue as best you can, folding two or three times consecutively if possible, until the dough looks and feels supple and strong. You may need to let the dough relax for 5 minutes in between folds, then flatten the dough and continue the process.

Fold the dough a second time, turn it over, and then fold a third time if possible.

FERMENT Oil a second large bowl, then place the dough in it, seam side up, to oil the top. Then turn it seam side down, and cover the bowl with oiled plastic wrap. Mark the time with a felt-tipped pen on the plastic wrap and allow the dough to rest and rise in a moderately cool place until it has doubled in volume, 1 to 2 hours, depending on the heat of your environment.

After the first 30 minutes of fermentation, turn the dough out of the bowl onto your work surface, and fold again as described on the previous page. Return the dough to the bowl, cover, and complete the fermentation.

PRE-SHAPE, REST, CUT, AND SHAPE Once the dough has doubled in volume, sprinkle a little more flour onto your work surface, then scrape the dough out onto it, letting the dough assume its natural shape. Tap your hands in flour, and gently flatten the dough into a large, even rectangle of approximately 12 by 8 inches and 1 inch thick, with the short side facing you.

Spread a handful of the olive mixture evenly across the dough and gently press it in. Repeat with the rest of the olives. Beginning with the end farthest from you, roll up the dough into a tight log. Tuck in the outer ends each time you roll. When you reach the end of the dough, seal the edge as you would a batard (see page 58), then cover the dough with plastic wrap and let rest for 10 minutes.

Use a metal bench scraper or a knife to cut the dough log into seventeen or eighteen 2-ounce pieces. Shape these pieces into rolls, following the instructions for a boule on pages 60 and 61, and place them on a lightly oiled baking sheet.

PROOF Cover the rolls with oiled plastic wrap and let proof until they have doubled in size, approximately 30 minutes.

While the dough is proofing, preheat the oven to 425°F, with a rack in the middle for baking and an empty pan for creating steam on the bottom of the oven. Have ready a spritzer filled with water near the oven and approximately 8 ounces of hot water to pour into the empty pan.

Stir together the coarse salt and the celery seeds in a small bowl. Measure the olive oil into a separate small bowl and set aside.

SCORE Once the rolls have approximately doubled in volume, brush a little olive oil on top of each one, then sprinkle with just a little of the salt–celery seed mixture. Dip a lame or straightedge razor in water, and score each roll with a simple X, approximately ½ inch deep.

BAKE Open the oven door, and, working quickly, slide the baking sheet with the rolls onto the middle rack, then pour the hot water into the empty pan below to create steam before quickly closing the oven door. After 1 minute, open the oven door and spritz around the dough with water, then close the door again.

Bake for 30 to 35 minutes, until the rolls brown evenly across the top.

COOL When the rolls have finished baking, remove them from the baking sheet and let them cool completely on a wire rack.

Organic Whole Wheat Bread with Kamut, Amaranth, and Millet Flour

MORE AND MORE BAKERS and those who love to eat are exploring a new frontier of ancient grains because they're delicious, healthy, and wholesome. Many of these grains are defined as "ancient" because they have been farmed for thousands and thousands of years—civilizations were built around them. In this recipe, we start with whole wheat flour (choose organic for an even more wholesome option) and a whole wheat and kamut poolish, add a soaker of whole amaranth grains, and then incorporate millet flour into the dough. However, since amaranth and millet do not contain gluten, they are used only in small proportions with other gluten-containing flours.

YIELD
Approximately 38 ounces dough;
2 spiral-shaped loaves

POOLISH (MAKES 8 OUNCES)

Active dry yeast	½ teaspoon
Warm water	4 ounces
Whole wheat flour	2 ounces
Kamut flour	2 ounces

SOAKER (MAKES 3.5 OUNCES)

Amaranth	1 ounce
Cold water	2.5 ounces

≫ Remember, a poolish needs time to ferment before you can proceed with the dough, anywhere from 2½ to 3 hours at room temperature.

Whole Wheat Bread

Active dry yeast	1 teaspoon
Table salt	2 teaspoons
Warm water	1.75 ounces
Whole wheat flour, preferably organic	8 ounces
Unbleached bread flour	6 ounces
Millet flour	2 ounces
Cool water	8 ounces
Poolish (page 197)	8 ounces
Soaker (page 197)	3.5 ounces
Vegetable oil	

Poolish

MEASURE AND WEIGH Measure the yeast and set it aside.

Weigh the warm water into a small bowl. The warm water should feel hot to the touch, between 105° and 115°F. Sprinkle the yeast on top of the water, stir to dissolve, and set aside.

Weigh the whole wheat and the Kamut flours and combine in a bowl, stir to mix together, then make a well in the center.

MIX Add the yeast mixture to the flour, and stir 3 or 4 turns, until all of the ingredients are incorporated. If your poolish seems dry, add 0.5 to 1 more ounce of water.

FERMENT Cover the bowl with plastic wrap and allow to ferment at room temperature for 2½ to 3 hours.

Soaker

MAKE THE SOAKER Weigh the amaranth and the cold water into a small saucepan with a lid. Bring to a boil, then lower the heat and simmer for 20 to 25 minutes, until all water has been absorbed. Put the mixture in a small bowl and let it cool completely before adding it to the dough.

≫ This particular poolish should be used immediately after it has doubled in volume, after 2½ to 3 hours, and not be held in the refrigerator overnight, due to the vulnerable nature of the flours and their lack of protein and gluten strength.

Whole Wheat Bread

MEASURE AND WEIGH Measure the yeast and the salt separately and set them aside.

Weigh the warm water into a small bowl. The warm water should feel hot to the touch, between 105° and 115°F. Sprinkle the yeast on top of the water, stir to dissolve, and set aside.

Weigh the wheat flour, bread flour, and millet flour, combine them in a large bowl, and mix together. Then sprinkle the salt on top of the flours, stir to incorporate, and make a well in the center.

Weigh the cool water into a bowl.

MIX First, combine the poolish and the soaker with the cool water, using your fingers to help break up the poolish to dissolve. Add the yeast mixture to the flour, stir 3 or 4 turns, and then, little by little, add the cool water with the poolish and the soaker. Mix with your hands for 2 to 3 minutes, until all of the ingredients are incorporated, the grit of the salt is dissolved, and the dough forms a rough and shaggy mass, and then stop.

LET THE DOUGH REST Cover the bowl with a kitchen towel or plastic wrap and let the dough stand still for about 30 minutes.

FOLD Sprinkle your work surface with flour and then use a plastic bowl scraper to scrape the dough out onto it. Tap your hands in a little flour, then gently flatten the dough into a rectangle, with the short side facing you.

Use your fingers or the plastic scraper to flip the top edge of the dough down to just below the center, then flip the bottom edge up to just above the center. Repeat this process for the right and left sides, then turn the dough over and dust off the flour.

FERMENT Oil a second large bowl, then place the dough in it, seam side up, to oil the top. Then turn it seam side down, and cover the bowl with oiled plastic wrap. Mark the time with a felt-tipped pen on

Remember, to find the accurate water temperature, you will need to factor in the poolish, so multiply as follows: 75 x 4 (because the poolish counts as the fourth factor) = 300. Now subtract the room temperature, flour temperature, poolish temperature, and friction factor (see page 17) to get the appropriate water temperature for your dough.

ANCIENT GRAINS

Kamut (a trademarked name) is a whole-grain flour made from Khorasan wheat (and which contains gluten). It is a direct descendant of emmer wheat and dates from the advent of agriculture in Mesopotamia. Kamut has a buttery, nutty flavor, absorbs water easily, and gives this dough a luxurious and smooth texture. As with many ancient grains it has a high protein content and is a natural energy booster.

Amaranth, a tiny round seed domesticated some 8,000 years ago in Mexico and Peru, is now cultivated around the world for its superb nutritional value and is also milled into flour.

Hulled millet, a small seed, can also be made into millet flour (which is what we use for this recipe). It is from the Far East, having been farmed 10,000 years ago in China. It is light in flavor and an excellent source of dietary fiber.

the plastic wrap and allow the dough to rest and rise in a moderately cool place until it has doubled in volume, 1 to 2 hours, depending on the heat of your environment.

After the first 30 minutes of fermentation, turn the dough out of the bowl onto your work surface, and fold a second time as described on the previous page. Return the dough to the bowl, cover, and complete the fermentation.

PRE-SHAPE AND SHAPE Once the dough has doubled in volume, sprinkle a little more flour onto your work surface, then scrape the dough out onto it, letting the dough assume its natural shape. Tap your hands in flour, and gently flatten the dough, then divide into 2 equal pieces.

Pre-shape each dough piece into a log, following the instructions on page 7. Shape each log into a baguette, following the instructions on pages 37 to 39, then shape each baguette into a tight coil, with all sides touching, and place the coils on an oiled baking sheet at least 3 or 4 inches apart.

PROOF Cover the dough with oiled plastic wrap and let proof for 30 to 45 minutes, or just until it is almost doubled in volume.

While the dough is proofing, preheat the oven to 480°F, with an empty pan for creating steam on the bottom of the oven. Have ready a spritzer filled with water near the oven and approximately 8 ounces of hot water to pour into the empty pan.

BAKE Open the oven door, and, working quickly, slide the pan with the coils onto the middle rack, then pour the hot water into the empty pan below to create steam before quickly closing the oven door. After 1 minute, open the oven door and spritz around the dough with water, then close the door again.

The bread should bake to a rich brown color in 35 to 45 minutes.

COOL When the bread has finished baking, let it cool completely on a wire rack.

⫸ Folding a second time will help strengthen the dough, necessary because this dough contains one flour that has no gluten.

OTHER SHAPES TO TRY

You could also choose to shape this dough into a couronne: Divide the dough into 18 or 19 two-ounce pieces and shape them into rolls, following the shaping instructions for a boule on pages 60 and 61. Proof, score, and bake as directed for the Couronne of White Rolls on page 134.

LAST

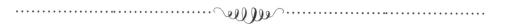

New earths, new themes expect us.
—Henry David Thoreau, *The Journal* (1857)

Over the past thirty years I've spent many summer days with my friend Polly, visiting her family, Pete and Mart Comstock, at their farm and home in upstate New York. There are ninety acres of land with woods, streams, blueberry patches, and an occasional bear. Most impressive is the elaborate organic garden that has grown a hundredfold since my first visit there in 1975. Pete and Mart's care and hard work have inspired in me the desire to always be a good steward of the land.

At one of our many dinners around the long wooden table in the kitchen, the conversation turned to farming and in particular growing wheat and rye. Mart's great-grandfather, who traveled from Germany to farm in the beautiful Palouse region of Washington State, arrived in the United States with seeds of rye from his own crops sewn into the hem of his jacket.

This regard for farming and the land is a passion that has been embraced in the last few years by many bakers and chefs who are more and more educated about how the grain cultivars, soil, climate, farmer, and miller all impact good bread. Dan Barber writes extensively about these ideas in his book *The Third Plate*, as does Amy Halloran in her book, *The New Bread Basket*.

At Flowers and Bread, my partners and I are collaborating with farmers in our region to grow and mill heritage wheat and grains with anticipation that our breads will reflect these dedicated and remarkable flavor profiles. I am evaluating wheat varieties and analyzing soils, ready to plunge my hands into the dirt—a new passion I have long waited to explore and one that will surely take my baking to the next level.

From the start of this book and throughout all of the chapters, how you have learned about making bread has also had something to do with passion. To guide your hands through the paces of this craft and to come out on the other side with a bread worth breaking and sharing is a strong and elemental experience. Now that you've completed all the lessons and the instructions are imprinted in your memory, the confidence you have gained will allow the space for more desire, more knowledge, and more baking. And as you learn you will discover that it really does take a lifetime to be a baker.

INDEX

Note: Page references in *italics* indicate photographs of completed recipes.

A

Amaranth
    about, 94, 199
    German Rye with a Seed and
        Grain Soaker, 93–98, *95*
    Kamut, and Millet Flour,
        Organic Whole Wheat
        Bread with, *196*, 197–200,
        201
Anchovies
    Classic Pissaladière, 145–46, *147*
Apples, Figs, and Raisins, Whole
    Wheat Sourdough with,
    185–90, *187*, *188*
Autolyse, 26–27

B

Baguette Dough with Poolish: Epis
    and Ficelles, 67–73, *68*, *71*
Baguette foundation breads
    Cinnamon-Raisin Pan Loaf,
    131–33, *133*

Country White Loaf, 128, *129–30*
Couronne of White Rolls,
    134–36, *135*
Pain de Mie, *ii*, 137–40, *138*
Baguettes
    history of, 62
    recipe for, *32*, 35–40, *41*
Baking sheets, 14
Baking stones, 15
Batards
    history of, 62
    shaping, 58
    Whole Wheat Sourdough,
    115–18, *116*
Biga
    about, 66
    Ciabatta Rolls with, 80–85,
    81, *82*
Boules
    history of, 62
    shaping, 60–61
    White Sourdough, 110–14, *111*
Bread-baking
    designing a schedule for, 34
    step one: organization, 25
    step two: measuring, 25
    step three: mixing, 25–27
    step four: kneading or folding,
    27–28

step five: fermentation, 28–29
step six: shaping, 29
step seven: proofing, 29–30
step eight: scoring, 30
step nine: baking, 30
step ten: cooling, 30
Bread-shaping
    cutting an epi, 59
    folding, 56–57
    shaping a batard, 58
    shaping a boule, 60–61
    shaping a filone, 57
Butter, Sweet, Italian Semolina Bread
    with, 99–103, *100*

C

Celery Seed Salt, Olives, and Lemon
    Zest, Sour Rye Rolls with,
    191–95, *193*
Cheese
    Crackers, 163–65, *164*
    Focaccia with Red Onion,
        Asiago, and Thyme, *148*,
        149–50
    Pizza, *160*, 161–62

G

H

I

K

Kamut
    about, 199
    Amaranth, and Millet Flour,
        Organic Whole Wheat Bread
        with, *196*, 197–200, *201*

L

Lame, 11
Lavender Honey, Whole Wheat
    Sandwich Bread with,
    166–68
Lemon
    Slices with Tarragon and
        Sea Salt, Focaccia with
        (variation), *viii*, 150, *151*
    Zest, Olives, and Celery Seed
        Salt, Sour Rye Rolls with,
        191–95, *193*
Loaf pans, 14

M

Measuring cups, 4
Metal and plastic scrapers, 11
Millet
    hulled, about, 199
    Kamut, and Amaranth Flour,
        Organic Whole Wheat
        Bread with, *196*, 197–200,
        201
Mixing bowls, 10

O

Olive paste
    Classic Pissaladière, 145–46, *147*
    Pizza, 160, *161–62*
Olives, Lemon Zest, and Celery Seed
    Salt, Sour Rye Rolls with,
    191–95, *193*
Onion(s)
    Classic Pissaladière, 145–46, *147*
    Red, Asiago, and Thyme,
        Focaccia with, *148*, 149–50
Organic Whole Wheat Bread with
    Kamut, Amaranth, and
    Millet Flour, *196*, 197–200,
    201

P

Pain de Campagne, French Whole
    Wheat, 87–92, *89*
Pain de Campagne, Whole Wheat,
    foundation breads
    Whole Wheat Rolls with
        Toasted Grains and
        Currants, 170–74
    Whole Wheat Sandwich Bread
        with Lavender Honey,
        166–68
Pain de Mie, *ii*, 137–40, *138*
Pan Loaves
    Cinnamon-Raisin, 131–33, *133*
    Country White Loaf, *128*,
        129–130

Pain de Mie, *ii*, 137–140, *138*
Rye Sourdough, 119–23, *121*, *122*
Whole Wheat Sandwich Bread
    with Lavender Honey,
    166–168
Whole Wheat Sourdough with
    Figs, Apples, and Raisins,
    185–190, *187*, *188*
Parchment paper, 14
Pâte Fermentée
    about, 65
    Focaccia Breadsticks with,
        74–79, *75*, *78*
Pecans, Toasted, Semolina Bread
    with, 183–84
Pissaladière, Classic, 145–46, *147*
Pizza, 160, *161–62*
Plastic and metal scrapers, 11
Pomegranate Crackers (variation),
    165
Poolish
    about, 65–66
    Baguette Dough with (Epis and
        Ficelles), 67–73, *68*, *71*
Preferments
    about, 27
    infusing breads with, 64–66
Pullman pans, 14
Pumpernickel, Rich, with Toasted
    Grains, 175–79, *176*